D0237004

Chicken

Chicken

Jeni Wright

hamlyn

Published in the UK in 1996
by Hamlyn, a division of Octopus Publishing Group Ltd
2–4 Heron Quays, London E14 4JP

This edition published 2001

ISBN 0 600 60573 6

Printed in China

NOTES

Both metric and imperial measurements have been given in all recipes. Use one set of measurements only and not a mixture of both.

Standard level spoon measurements are used in all recipes.
1 tablespoon = one 15 ml spoon
1 teaspoon = one 5 ml spoon
Eggs should be size 3 unless otherwise stated.

Milk should be full fat unless otherwise stated.

Pepper should be freshly ground black pepper unless otherwise stated.

Fresh herbs should be used, unless otherwise stated. If unavailable, use dried herbs as an alternative but halve the quantities stated.

Measurements for canned food have been given as a standard metric equivalent.

Ovens should be preheated to the specified temperature – if using a fan-assisted oven, follow the manufacturer's instructions for adjusting the time and the temperature.

To test if poultry is cooked, pierce the flesh through the thickest part with a skewer or fork – the juices should run clear, never pink or red.

TURKEY THAWING AND COOKING GUIDE

WEIGHT	NUMBER OF SERVINGS	THAWING TIME IN A COOL ROOM (BELOW 15°C/60°F)	COOKING TIME AT 190°C (375°F), GAS MARK 5 WITHOUT FOIL	COOKING TIME AT 190°C (375°F), GAS MARK 5 WITH FOIL
1.4-2.25 kg/3-5 lb	4–6	20 hrs	1½–1¾ hrs	1¾–2 hrs
2.75-3.25 kg/6-7 lb	7–9	30 hrs	1¾–2 hrs	2–2¼ hrs
3.5-4 kg/8-9 lb	10–14	36 hrs	2–2½ hrs	2½–2¾ hrs
4.5-5 kg/10-11 lb	15–16	45 hrs	2¼–2¾ hrs	2½–3 hrs
5.5-6 kg/12-13 lb	17–18	48 hrs	2¾–3 hrs	3–3¼ hrs
6.5-8 kg/14-17 lb	19–25	48 hrs	3¼–3½ hrs	3½–3¾ hrs
8.5-12 kg/18-22 lb	26–37	48 hrs	3½–3¾ hrs	3¾–4 hrs
12.5 kg plus/23 lb plus	38 plus	48 hrs	3¾ hrs plus	4¼ hrs plus

Contents

Introduction

Poultry meat is quick, versatile and easy to cook, and its quality and flavour are so good it is almost impossible not to make it into a delicious meal, no matter how simple. Chicken and turkey are the two most popular types of poultry, with duck tending to be reserved for special occasions, and goose eaten mostly at Christmas time or Easter.

CHICKEN

The best chickens are free-range – more expensive than the battery-farm kind, but full of flavour, succulent and tender. However, if cost is a major consideration, all poultry, free-range or not, is still very good value.

Whole Chickens

These are generally labelled 'oven ready', and weigh anything from 500 g/1 lb–3.5 kg/7 lb. They can be roasted, pot-roasted, poached or braised. Look for a plump, pliable breast with fairly moist (but not wet) skin, and no broken or dark patches.

To check if a whole chicken is cooked through, pierce between the leg and thigh with a fork or fine skewer. The juices should run clear with no trace of pink or red.

Poussins

The smallest chickens, no more than 4–6 weeks old, very tender and quick to cook. Cook them whole for 1 person, or spatchcocked for 2.

Spring Chickens

Up to 12 weeks old, weighing about 1.25 kg/2½ lb, giving 2–3 servings.

Larger Chickens

Older, larger birds are rare these days, and smaller chickens must be substituted when making stocks, soups and broths, and in old recipes calling for 'boiling fowl'.

Chicken Breasts

Bone-in breasts are easy to cook. The bone keeps the meat moist and juicy and prevents overcooking; it slips out easily after cooking.

Suprêmes are boneless chicken breasts with part of the wing bone attached, a speciality cut often used by professional chefs. Any other type of breast may be used instead.

Breasts are also available boneless, with or without skin. The latter is often labelled 'fillet' or 'escalope' if it has been sliced and/or pounded thin.

All breast meat is top-quality lean meat that cooks very quickly – the ultimate convenience food, suitable for pan-frying, sautéing, grilling, barbecuing, poaching, steaming and stir-frying.

Thighs and Drumsticks

Less expensive than breast meat, and better for dishes such as casseroles and stews with long cooking times.

DUCK

Duck is fattier and bonier than chicken or turkey, but is now bred leaner, with a higher proportion of meat to bone.

Whole Birds

Ducklings (to 8 weeks old) and ducks (over 8 weeks) are best roasted

JOINTS AND BREASTS
Best for roasting and casseroling. Boneless breasts, or 'magrets', rich and meaty, are available in good butchers and some supermarkets, and make marvellous dinner party fare. They can be roasted, pan-fried, sautéed, grilled and barbecued.

TURKEY

Now available year round, turkey is lean, nutritious and economical. Its rather bland flavour is good with strong-tasting vegetables, herbs and spices to pep up the taste.

WHOLE TURKEYS
Best roasted (see the chart on page 4 for oven temperatures and cooking times according to size).

TURKEY JOINTS
Legs, thighs and breasts, bone-in or boneless, sometimes rolled and stuffed, or butter-basted. They are all convenient and good-quality.

BONELESS TURKEY BREAST
Versatile and inexpensive, available thinly sliced as steaks and escalopes, it can be used in any recipe for chicken that calls for boneless breast.

MINCED TURKEY
A low-fat alternative to minced beef.

BONING A WHOLE BIRD

A boned bird makes a wonderful natural casing for a stuffing, joint of meat or another bird. Neat and very easy to carve, this is a special boon at Christmas time, when a large number of people need to be served with hot turkey at the same time (see page 94). Boned, stuffed and rolled birds are also good for buffets and large parties where people help themselves – and they are even easier to carve when served cold.

If just the cavity and breast of the bird are boned, this can be stuffed and reformed back into shape, so that it looks like a conventional bird when cooked (see steps 1–8). You could also bone the whole bird (steps 9–11 on page 8), including the legs and wings, to make a classic ballotine or galantine. A boning knife with a 12–15 cm/5–6 inch blade will make boning easy.

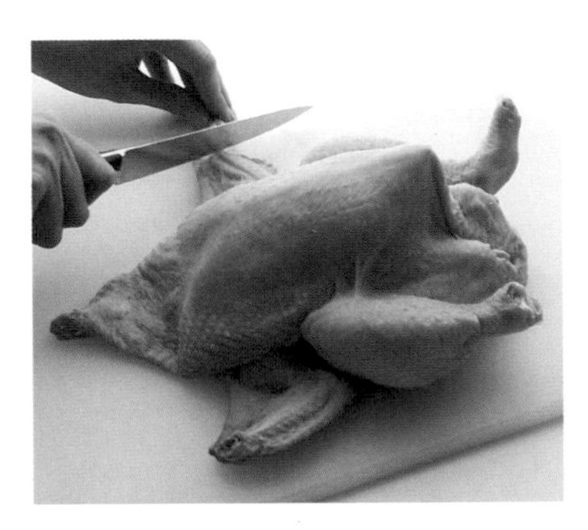

1 Cut off the ends of the legs and wings at the first joints and remove the wishbone as described below.
2 To remove the wishbone, lift back the neck skin from the bird and cut away the flesh from around the wishbone with the point of a small sharp knife, keeping as close to the bone as possible. Cut out the wishbone and remove any surrounding fat. It is advisable to remove the wishbone in this way even when you are dealing with whole birds, since it will make the bird easier to carve.

3 Place the bird with the breast side down on the board, and cut along the backbone, working from the tail to neck end.

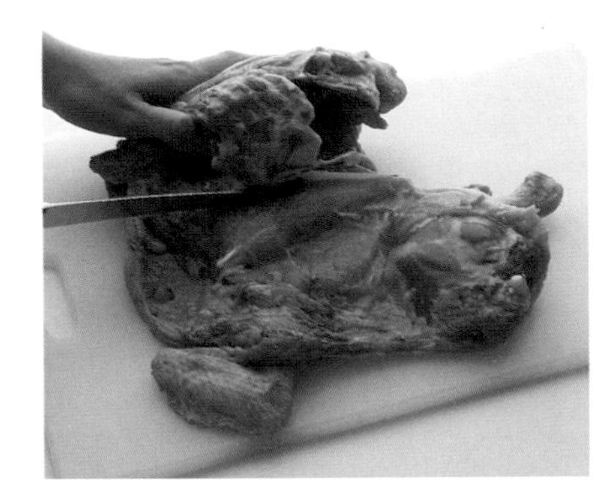

4 Holding the knife blade angled towards the carcass, carefully scrape away the flesh from the rib cage, working down one side of the bird until the wing is reached.
5 Ease the knife between the ball and socket joint and sever from the rib cage, while keeping it attached to the skin.
6 Continue easing away the flesh from the bone, using small scraping cuts, until you reach the leg joint. Then sever the ball and socket joint in the

same way as the wing. Continue in this way until you have reached the ridge of the breastbone.
7 Turn the chicken around and repeat in exactly the same way on the other side of the bird.
8 Pull very gently and carefully to separate the breastbone from the skin. You will find that there is no flesh on the bird at this point, and you must therefore take care not to tear the fragile skin along the ridge of the breastbone, or the bird will split open while it is cooking. When you are boning a chicken, it is a good idea to keep all the bones and trimmings to one side so that you can use them later for making a really good stock.

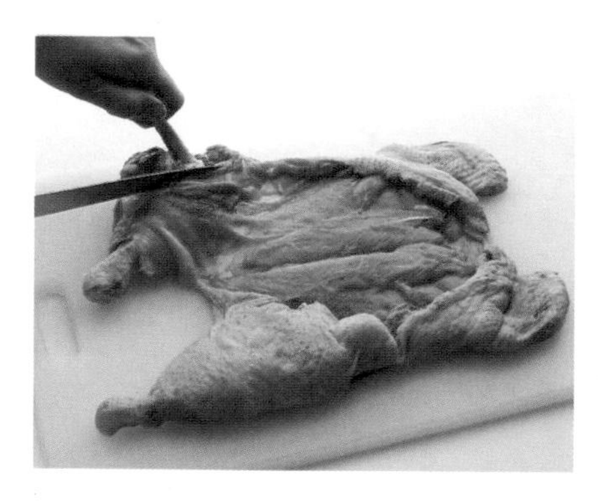

9 Lay the chicken flat on the board, with the skin side facing down. Hold the outside of a wing bone in one hand and, with the knife in the other, carefully scrape away the flesh from the wing bone. Work from top to bottom, and sever all the tendons as you go. Pull out the wing bone. Repeat in the same way with other wing. Push the skin and flesh of the wings back inside the carcass so as to make a neater parcel for stuffing.

10 Hold inside of leg bone and scrape away the flesh with a pencil-sharpening action. Sever tendons as you go, then release the bone when you get to bottom of leg. Repeat with other leg.

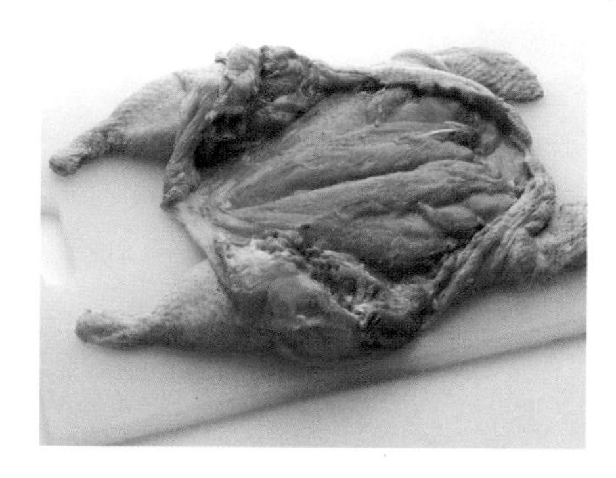

11 After boning, the bird is ready to receive the chosen stuffing.

JOINTING A BIRD

The only equipment needed is a large chef's knife which should be very sharp and clean. You can use poultry shears too, but these are not essential.

1 Place the bird breast-side down and cut around the oyster meat on either side of the backbone to expose it.
2 Turn the bird breast-side up and cut down between the leg and the body. Twist sharply to break the ball and socket joint, then cut to release the leg, keeping the oyster meat attached to the leg. Repeat with the other leg.
3 Cut along both sides of the breastbone, spread the bird open and cut along each side of the backbone (with poultry shears if you have them) and remove.
4 Cut off the knuckle ends of the drumsticks and the wing tips.
5 You now have 4 joints. For 8 joints, cut each diagonally in half. Include some breast meat with each wing. Cut legs through knee joints.

MAKING STOCK

Stock is an essential ingredient in many dishes, especially soups, casseroles and stews. Stock cubes rarely have the depth of flavour of a well-made stock and are often very salty. You can buy cartons of freshly made chicken stock at many large supermarkets. These are infinitely better than stock cubes, but there really is no substitute for making your own.

Make a large quantity and freeze in usable amounts (it will keep in the freezer for up to 3 months). To save space, boil it down until reduced, then freeze in ice cube trays to make concentrated stock cubes. Pack them in freezer bags, and when you need chicken stock, drop a frozen cube into hot liquid to dissolve it.

CHICKEN STOCK USING A FRESH BIRD

Boiling fowls, once used for this kind of stock, are rare now. An ordinary oven-ready bird may be substituted.

Do not include the chicken liver

when making stock or the finished stock will have a bitter taste. Use very little salt; seasoning can be adjusted later in the final dish. If too much salt is used in the making of the stock it cannot be reduced later.

1 Put 1 x 1 kg/2 lb chicken (giblets removed) in a large saucepan with 2.4 litres/4 pints water, add the giblets (except the liver), 1 onion and 1 carrot, both quartered, 1–2 celery sticks, sliced, 1 large bouquet garni, 6 black peppercorns and a pinch of salt. Bring to the boil, skimming the scum as it rises to the surface.
2 Lower the heat, half cover the pan and simmer gently for 3 hours. Skim and top up with water as necessary.
3 Remove the bird and strain stock into a bowl. Blot off any surface fat with paper towels and use the stock immediately, or leave until cold, cover and refrigerate for up to 3 days. Remove any solidified fat.

STOCK USING BONES OR A CARCASS

Raw bones and trimmings left after boning or jointing can be used for stock, so too can a carcass leftover after cooking.

1 Break the carcass or raw bones in pieces and put in a large saucepan. Add leftover stuffing and giblets (except the liver), 1.75 litres/3 pints water, 2 celery sticks, sliced, 1 leek and 1 carrot, both quartered lengthways, 1 bouquet garni and a pinch of salt. Bring to the boil and skim off the scum as it rises to the surface.
2 Lower the heat, half cover the pan with a lid and simmer gently for 3 hours, skimming and topping up with water as necessary.
3 Carefully strain the stock through a large sieve or colander into a bowl. Blot off any surface fat with paper towels and use as in previous recipe.

GIBLET STOCK

Giblets make good stock for gravy, but do not include the liver. French cooks chop the liver finely and add it to the pan juices with stock to make a sauce for roast chicken, but if you find this too strong, save the liver for another use.

1 Put chicken or turkey giblets (except the liver) in a pan with 1.15 litres/2 pints water. Add 1 small onion stuck with 2–3 cloves, 1 carrot, quartered lengthways and 1 celery stick, sliced. Bring to the boil and skim off the scum as it rises to the surface.
2 Lower the heat, cover the pan and simmer gently for 2 hours. Strain the stock into a jug or bowl and proceed as in the recipe on page 8.

POULTRY AND YOUR HEALTH

White poultry meat is a healthy alternative to red meat, an excellent, economical source of protein, low in fat and cholesterol, and a good source of vitamin B.

1 To reduce fat content, remove the skin before cooking. Skin helps keep poultry moist during cooking, however, so you may wish to leave it on for cooking but remove it before serving.
2 Raw poultry can contain low levels of salmonella and campylobacter bacteria, responsible for food poisoning. If poultry is stored and handled correctly and cooked thoroughly, bacteria will be rendered harmless. To test if cooked, pierce the flesh in the thickest part with a fork – the juices should run clear, not pink or red.
3 Fresh raw poultry should be eaten as soon as possible, or refrigerated and eaten within 2 days or according to packet instructions. Always remove plastic bags and polystyrene trays, place the chicken on a rack over a plate and cover loosely with foil. The rack prevents the bird from sitting in juices that may harbour bacteria. Remove and store giblets separately, unwrapped, in a covered bowl.
4 Completely thaw frozen birds at a cool room temperature before cooking. If any ice crystals remain, birds may not cook thoroughly and any bacteria may not be killed – important for large birds (see page 4 for thawing times). Never refreeze raw poultry once it has been thawed.
5 Hands, utensils and work surfaces must be scrupulously clean before preparing poultry, and never prepare raw and cooked poultry at the same time. Before cooking, wipe raw poultry with paper towels – very important with the cavities of whole birds which may harbour bacteria.
6 Never stuff the cavity of a bird; stuff the neck end only or, better still, bake the stuffing in a separate dish. If bacteria are present in the bird's juices, these could drip into the stuffing, and the stuffing may prevent the bird from being thoroughly cooked.

Quick and Easy

Sauté of Chicken with Garlic, Lemon and Herbs

3 garlic cloves, chopped
4 tablespoons virgin olive oil
4 chicken portions
finely grated zest and juice of 1 lemon
1 tablespoon chopped fresh flat leaf parsley
2 teaspoons chopped fresh tarragon
salt and pepper

TO GARNISH:
lemon slices or twists
fresh herbs

1 Sauté the garlic in the oil until lightly coloured but not browned.
2 Add the chicken in a single layer, season to taste and sauté, turning frequently, for 15–20 minutes until the skin is crisp and golden brown.
3 Lower the heat, cover the pan and continue cooking for 15–20 minutes until the juices run clear when the thickest part of a portion is pierced with a skewer or fork.
4 Remove the chicken from the pan with a slotted spoon and place on a warmed serving platter.
5 Add the lemon zest and juice to the pan and stir well until sizzling to dislodge any sediment in the bottom of the pan.
6 Remove from the heat and add the herbs and salt and pepper to taste. Stir well to mix, then pour over the chicken. Serve hot, garnished with lemon slices and fresh herbs. A crisp green or mixed salad and French fries would make suitable accompaniments.

Serves 4
Preparation time: 10 minutes
Cooking time: 30–40 minutes

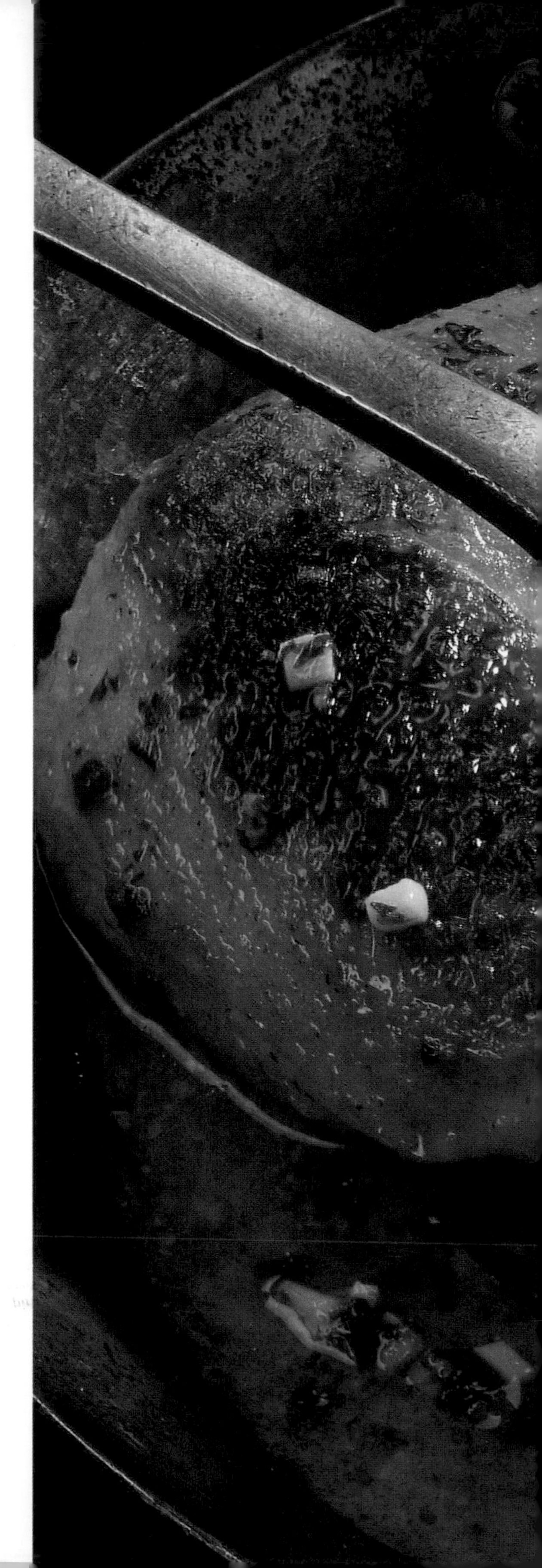

Lemon Chicken

This classic Chinese dish, originally from Hong Kong, appears on the menu in most Chinese restaurants.

- **1 egg white**
- **2 teaspoons cornflour**
- **500 g/1 lb skinless chicken breast fillets, cut diagonally into thin strips**
- **75 ml/3 fl oz rapeseed oil**
- **salt**
- **very finely chopped spring onions or strips of lemon zest, to garnish**

SAUCE:

- **2 teaspoons cornflour**
- **6 tablespoons cold Chicken Stock (see pages 8–9)**
- **1 garlic clove, crushed**
- **2 tablespoons lemon juice**
- **1 tablespoon soy sauce**
- **2 teaspoons rice wine or dry sherry**
- **1 teaspoon caster sugar**
- **finely grated zest of ½ lemon**

1 Whisk the egg white lightly with a fork just to break it up. Add the cornflour and a pinch of salt, and whisk to mix. Add the chicken, turn gently to coat, and set aside.
2 To prepare the sauce, blend the cornflour with 2 tablespoons cold chicken stock in a jug, then blend in the remaining stock and sauce ingredients. Set the sauce aside.
3 Heat a wok or large deep frying pan until hot. Add the oil and heat over a moderate heat until hot but not smoking. Add the strips of chicken, a few at a time, and stir immediately in the oil to prevent them from sticking. Stir-fry for 2–3 minutes until golden and crisp, then remove with a slotted spoon and drain on paper towels.
4 Pour the oil out of the wok. Whisk the sauce, then pour into the wok. Increase the heat to high and bring to the boil, stirring constantly. Simmer for 1–2 minutes, stirring.
5 Lower the heat and return the chicken to the wok. Stir-fry for 2–3 minutes, and check seasoning.
6 Serve immediately, sprinkled with finely chopped spring onions or strips of lemon zest, and accompanied by steamed or boiled white rice and a stir-fried green vegetable such as finely sliced cabbage.

Serves 3–4
Preparation time: 10 minutes
Cooking time: 15 minutes

Chicken and Mangetout in Black Bean Sauce

Presentation is all important in Chinese cooking, so cut the chicken and vegetables into thin strips the same length as the mangetout.

- **3 tablespoons rapeseed oil**
- **1 red pepper, cored, deseeded and cut lengthways into very thin strips**
- **2 celery sticks, cut into very thin lengthways strips**
- **2.5 cm/1 inch piece of fresh root ginger, cut into very thin strips**
- **2 garlic cloves, crushed**
- **125 g/4 oz small mangetout**
- **500 g/1 lb skinless chicken breast fillets, cut diagonally into thin strips**
- **4 tablespoons black bean sauce**
- **4 tablespoons water**
- **salt and pepper**

1 Heat 2 tablespoons of the oil in a wok or large, deep frying pan until hot but not smoking. Add the red pepper, celery, ginger and garlic and stir-fry over a gentle heat for 3–4 minutes until the vegetables are just softened but not coloured.
2 Add the mangetout and stir-fry for a further minute, taking care that they are still crisp and crunchy. Remove all the vegetables with a slotted spoon and set aside.
3 Heat the remaining oil in the wok, add the chicken and stir-fry over a moderate heat for 3–4 minutes.

4 Add the black bean sauce and the water and stir-fry for a further 2–3 minutes until the chicken is tender when pierced with a skewer or fork.
5 Return the stir-fried vegetables to the wok and toss for 1–2 minutes until all of the ingredients are evenly mixed and piping hot. Add salt and pepper to taste. Serve immediately, with Chinese egg noodles or steamed or boiled white rice.

Serves 4
Preparation time: 10 minutes
Cooking time: 10–15 minutes

Chicken Bang Bang

In authentic Chinese recipes, this dish is made with a whole chicken, but using chicken thighs, as here, is much easier. The term 'bang bang' comes from the fact that the whole chicken was 'banged' after cooking, with a heavy implement, to break the chicken up into pieces.

- **12 chicken thighs**
- **2.5 cm/1 inch piece of fresh root ginger, chopped roughly**
- **1 hot green chilli, deseeded and chopped finely**
- **4 tablespoons soy sauce**
- **900 ml/1½ pints water**
- **3 carrots, cut into very thin matchstick strips**
- **½ cucumber, cut into very thin matchstick strips**
- **1 large green pepper, cored, deseeded and cut lengthways into very thin matchstick strips**
- **125 g/4 oz bean sprouts**
- **2 tablespoons sesame seeds**
- **3 tablespoons rice wine or dry sherry**
- **2 tablespoons sesame oil**
- **2 tablespoons clear honey**

1 Put the chicken thighs in a saucepan with the chopped ginger and chilli, half the soy sauce and the water. Bring to the boil over a moderate heat, then cover and simmer over a gentle heat for about 40 minutes until the chicken is tender when pierced with either a skewer or fork. Remove from the heat and leave the chicken to cool in the cooking liquid for about 2 hours.
2 Remove the chicken thighs from the liquid and 'bang' them with a rolling pin to release the meat from the bones. Discard the bones and skin and cut the chicken into strips. Strain the cooking liquid and reserve.
3 Put the chicken strips in a bowl with the carrots, cucumber, green pepper and bean sprouts. Fold gently to mix and set aside.
4 Put the sesame seeds in a small heavy-bottomed or non-stick frying pan. Dry-fry over a gentle heat, stirring constantly, for 2–3 minutes until toasted. Do not overcook.
5 Stir in the rice wine or sherry, sesame oil, remaining soy sauce, honey and a few tablespoons of the reserved cooking liquid. Heat through gently, stirring frequently, until evenly blended.
6 Pour the sesame seed mixture over the chicken and vegetables. Toss well to mix, then cover and marinate in the refrigerator for at least 4 hours, preferably overnight, turning the chicken and vegetables occasionally. Serve at room temperature on a bed of lettuce, for a first course or a light lunch dish.

Serves 4
Preparation time: 20 minutes, plus marinating
Cooking time: about 40 minutes

Chilli Chicken

This quick, Indonesian-style curry tastes even better if left to stand overnight and reheated the next day.

- **3 tablespoons rapeseed oil**
- **1 small onion, chopped finely**
- **2.5 cm/1 inch piece of fresh root ginger, chopped finely**
- **2 garlic cloves, crushed**
- **12 skinned and boned chicken thighs, cut into bite-sized pieces**
- **2 tablespoons crunchy peanut butter**
- **2–3 tablespoons hot water**
- **2 tablespoons chilli sauce**
- **1–2 teaspoons chilli powder, according to taste**
- **1 teaspoon dark soft brown sugar**
- **1 x 400 ml/14 fl oz can coconut milk**
- **¼ teaspoon salt**

TO GARNISH:

- **chilli flowers or rings**
- **chopped roasted peanuts, toasted coconut and chopped fresh coriander**

1 Heat the oil in a large flameproof casserole, add the onion, ginger and garlic and fry over a gentle heat, stirring, for about 5 minutes until softened but not coloured.

2 Add the chicken, increase the heat to moderate and cook, stirring, for 7–10 minutes, until it changes colour on all sides.

3 Mix the peanut butter and water, then add to the chicken with the chilli sauce, chilli powder and sugar. Stir well to mix for 1–2 minutes.

4 Add the coconut milk and bring to the boil, stirring. Add the salt, cover and simmer over a gentle heat, stirring occasionally, for 20 minutes or until the chicken is tender.

5 Serve hot, garnished with chilli flowers or rings and chopped peanuts, toasted coconut and fresh coriander. Steamed or boiled white rice is the only accompaniment you will need with this dish. Serve it with chilled Asian beer.

Serves 4

Preparation time: 10 minutes

Cooking time: about 30 minutes

Chicken Marsala

The combination of Marsala wine, balsamic vinegar and mascarpone is absolutely heavenly – in both taste and texture. This is just about the perfect dish for entertaining at very short notice.

- **1 tablespoon virgin olive oil**
- **50 g/2 oz butter**
- **6 part-boned chicken breasts, skinned**
- **1 head of garlic, broken into cloves**
- **2 tablespoons balsamic vinegar**
- **175 ml/6 fl oz Marsala**
- **175 ml/6 fl oz hot Chicken Stock (see pages 8–9)**
- **4 tablespoons mascarpone**
- **salt and pepper**
- **fresh tarragon leaves, to garnish**

1 Heat the olive oil and butter in a large flameproof casserole. Then add the chicken and whole unpeeled garlic cloves and sauté over a moderate heat for 7–10 minutes until the chicken has turned a pale golden colour on all sides.

2 Spoon the balsamic vinegar over the chicken, let it bubble for 1–2 minutes, then pour in the Marsala and stock and add salt and pepper to taste. Lower the heat, cover and simmer for 20 minutes or until the chicken is tender when pierced with a skewer or fork. Turn the breasts over and baste them with the sauce halfway through.

3 Remove the chicken with a slotted spoon and keep warm. Tip the contents of the pan into a sieve set over a bowl and let the cooking liquid strain through. With the back of a spoon, press the garlic flesh through the sieve into the liquid, slipping off the skins.

4 Return the liquid to the pan, then add the mascarpone and bring to the boil, stirring. Boil for 5-7 minutes or until the sauce is reduced to a coating consistency. Taste for seasoning and adjust if necessary.

5 Arrange the chicken on warmed dinner plates and spoon over the sauce. Serve hot, garnished with fresh tarragon leaves. Boiled new potatoes and a plain green vegetable such as courgettes, broccoli or mangetout would make suitable accompaniments for this dish.

Serves 6

Preparation time: 15 minutes
Cooking time: about 30 minutes

Spicy Chicken Casserole

Cinnamon, cloves and coriander give this casserole a subtle perfume. Here it is made with chicken stock. For a special occasion add red wine instead of the stock, or use half wine and half stock, to give a fuller flavour.

- **2 tablespoons plain flour**
- **1 teaspoon ground coriander**
- **½ teaspoon ground cinnamon**
- **¼ teaspoon ground cloves**
- **4 chicken portions, skinned**
- **3 tablespoons virgin olive oil**
- **2 celery sticks, chopped finely**
- **1 onion, chopped finely**
- **2 garlic cloves, crushed**
- **1 x 425 g/14 oz can chopped or crushed tomatoes**
- **1 tablespoon tomato purée**
- **300 ml/½ pint hot Chicken Stock (see pages 8–9)**
- **2–3 tablespoons chopped fresh coriander**
- **salt and pepper**

1 Spread the flour out on a plate. Add the coriander, cinnamon, cloves and salt and pepper to taste and mix thoroughly, then use to coat the chicken.
2 Heat 2 tablespoons of the oil in a large flameproof casserole, add the chicken and sauté over a moderate heat for 7–10 minutes until golden on all sides. Remove with a slotted spoon and set aside on a plate.
3 Heat the remaining oil in the casserole, add the celery, onion and garlic and fry over a moderate heat, stirring frequently, for about 5 minutes until the vegetables are softened but not coloured.
4 Add the can of tomatoes and the tomato purée and stir well to mix with the onion, then add the stock. Increase the heat and bring to the boil, stirring to break up the tomatoes as much as possible.
5 Return the chicken to the casserole with the juices that have collected on the plate. Cover and simmer over a gentle heat, stirring occasionally, for 40 minutes or until the chicken is tender when pierced in the thickest part with a skewer or fork.
6 Gently stir in the chopped fresh coriander, taste for seasoning and adjust if necessary. Serve the casserole hot, with either plain boiled rice or boiled new potatoes.

Serves 4
Preparation time: 15 minutes
Cooking time: about 50 minutes

Somerset Chicken

Dry cider makes a good, flavoursome sauce, but if you prefer not to use alcohol you can use apple juice instead. Make sure to cut the carrots in thick slices so that they remain quite crunchy after cooking. If you are making this dish for children, who will love the subtle flavour of the sauce, take the meat off the bone after cooking and cut it into easy bite-sized pieces. This dish is also good served as a fricassée in a circle of rice.

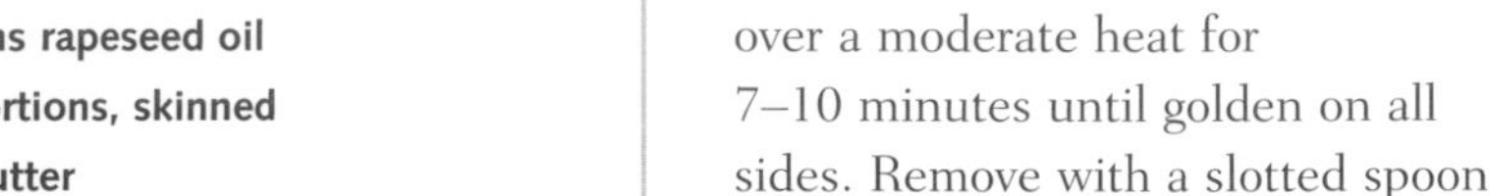

- **2 tablespoons rapeseed oil**
- **4 chicken portions, skinned**
- **15 g/½ oz butter**
- **2–3 celery sticks, chopped roughly**
- **1 large onion, chopped roughly**
- **2 tablespoons plain flour**
- **good pinch of mustard powder**
- **450 ml/¾ pint hot Chicken Stock (see pages 8–9)**
- **450 ml/¾ pint dry cider**
- **500 g/1 lb carrots, sliced thickly**
- **1 large bouquet garni**
- **salt and pepper**
- **fresh bay leaves and/or thyme, to garnish**

1 Heat the oil in a large flameproof casserole, add the chicken and sauté over a moderate heat for 7–10 minutes until golden on all sides. Remove with a slotted spoon and set aside on a plate.

2 Melt the butter in the casserole, add the celery and onion and cook over a gentle heat, stirring frequently, for about 5 minutes until softened but not coloured.

3 Add the flour and mustard powder, stir well to mix with the celery and onion, then cook for 1-2 minutes, stirring constantly. Gradually stir in the stock and cider and bring to the boil, stirring all the time.

4 Add the carrots, bouquet garni and salt and pepper to taste, then return the chicken to the casserole with any juices that have collected on the plate.

5 Bring the liquid to the boil again, then cover the casserole and place in a preheated oven, 180°C (350°F), Gas Mark 4 for 40 minutes or until the chicken is tender when pierced in the thickest part with a skewer or fork. Turn the chicken portions over halfway during the cooking time, to ensure they are covered in liquid and cook evenly.

6 Remove and discard the bouquet garni. Taste for seasoning. Serve hot, garnished with bay leaves and/or thyme. Creamed potatoes and a fresh green vegetable such as broccoli would make good accompaniments.

Serves 4

Preparation time: 20 minutes

Cooking time: 40 minutes

Oven temperature: 180°C (350°F), Gas Mark 4

Crispy Cheesy Chicken

Plain crisps and Cheddar cheese are used here, but you can experiment with different flavours and varieties of both crisps and cheese to suit your family's taste. For instance, sour cream and chive crisps mixed with Red Leicester cheese is a favourite with teenagers. To crush crisps quickly, put them in a heavy-duty polythene bag and crush lightly with a rolling pin.

- **75 g/3 oz plain crisps, crushed**
- **125 g/4 oz Cheddar cheese, grated**
- **1 teaspoon dried mixed herbs**
- **65 g/2½ oz butter**
- **4 chicken portions, skinned**
- **½ teaspoon paprika**
- **pepper**

1 Mix the crushed crisps, cheese and herbs together in a bowl. Add pepper to taste.
2 Melt the butter in a small saucepan. Use a little melted butter to brush the inside of an ovenproof dish into which the chicken portions will fit in a single layer. Arrange the chicken portions in the dish and brush all over with half the remaining melted butter.
3 Press the cheese mixture over the chicken, then drizzle over the remaining melted butter and sprinkle with the paprika.
4 Put the dish in a preheated oven, 180°C (350°F), Gas Mark 4 for 45 minutes until the juices run clear when the thickest part of a portion is pierced with either a skewer or fork. Serve hot, with a tomato and onion ring salad.

Serves 4
Preparation time: 10 minutes
Cooking time: about 45 minutes
Oven temperature: 180°C (350°F), Gas Mark 4

Chicken and Sweet Pepper Kebabs

Try to cut the chicken, onion and red pepper into chunks of roughly the same size. This gives the kebabs a neat appearance and helps ensure even cooking.

- **150 ml/¼ pint natural yogurt**
- **2 tablespoons virgin olive oil**
- **2 garlic cloves, crushed**
- **2 tablespoons chopped fresh coriander**
- **2 teaspoon ground cumin**
- **8 skinned and boned chicken thighs, cut into large chunks**
- **1 onion, cut into chunks**
- **1 red pepper, cored, deseeded and cut into chunks**
- **1 green pepper, cored, deseeded and cut into chunks**
- **salt and pepper**

1 Mix the yogurt, oil, garlic, coriander and cumin together in a shallow dish with salt and pepper to taste. Add the cubes of chicken and stir well to mix. Cover and marinate at room temperature for 30–60 minutes.
2 Thread the cubes of chicken on to kebab skewers, alternating them with pieces of onion and red and green pepper.
3 Put the kebabs on the rack of the grill pan. Place under a preheated hot grill and cook, turning frequently, for 20 minutes or until the chicken is tender when pierced with a skewer or fork. Serve hot, on a bed of saffron rice and accompanied by a raita of yogurt, cucumber and chopped fresh coriander.

Serves 4
Preparation time: 15 minutes, plus marinating
Cooking time: 20 minutes

VARIATION

Yakitori Chicken

Yakitori is the Japanese version of kebabs – cook the skewered chicken under the grill, or over hot coals on the barbecue for an authentic charred look.

1 Crush a 5 cm/2 inch piece of root ginger to a paste with 4 garlic cloves and 8 black peppercorns.
2 Place 150 ml/¼ pint Japanese soy sauce (shoyu), 150 m/¼ pint rice wine (sake), 2 tablespoons soft brown sugar and 1 tablespoon oil in a dish. Add the ginger and garlic paste and whisk to combine.
3 Cut 500 g/1 lb skinless chicken breast fillets diagonally into thin strips. Add to the marinade and stir well to mix. Cover and marinate at room temperature for at least 30 minutes. Meanwhile, soak 16 bamboo skewers in warm water.
4 Drain the skewers, then thread the chicken strips on to them, and place under a preheated hot grill for 8–10 minutes until the chicken is tender. Turn the skewers and baste the chicken with the marinade frequently during the cooking time. Serve hot, garnished with spring onion tassels.

Serves 4
Preparation time: 15 minutes, plus marinating
Cooking time: 8–10 minutes

Chicken and Pasta Salad with Roquefort Dressing

If you are fond of roasted peppers, you can roast the peppers for this salad. Follow the instructions for Chicken Suprêmes with Roast Peppers (page 82). Roquefort is an expensive cheese so you could use Gorgonzola or Dolcelatte instead.

- **1 tablespoon virgin olive oil**
- **250 g/8 oz small pasta shapes (e.g. spirals, bows or shells)**
- **250 g/8 oz skinned and boned cooked chicken, diced**
- **1 red pepper, cored, deseeded and chopped finely**
- **1 yellow or orange pepper, cored, deseeded and chopped finely**
- **salt and pepper**

DRESSING:

- **50 g/2 oz Roquefort cheese**
- **2 tablespoons virgin olive oil**
- **2 tablespoons mayonnaise**
- **2 teaspoons white wine vinegar**

TO FINISH:

- **1–2 tablespoons chopped fresh herbs**
- **a few pitted black olives**

1 Bring a large saucepan of water to the boil, swirl in the oil and add ½ teaspoon salt. Add the pasta shapes and boil, uncovered, over a moderate heat for 10 minutes, or according to packet instructions, until al dente.
2 Meanwhile, make the dressing. Put the Roquefort in a large bowl and mash with a fork. Add the remaining dressing ingredients and whisk well until emulsified and thick.
3 Drain the pasta, turn into the bowl of dressing and toss well to coat. Add the chicken and seasoning, toss again until the ingredients are combined, then leave to cool.
4 Add the chopped peppers and herbs to the salad and toss well. Transfer the salad to a serving bowl and garnish with the olives. Serve at room temperature.

Serves 4–6
Preparation time: 20 minutes, plus cooling
Cooking time: about 10 minutes

Chicken Waldorf

Chicken or leftover Christmas turkey goes really well in this classic American salad. Add the apples to the mayonnaise immediately after dicing or they will discolour.

- **125 ml/4 fl oz mayonnaise**
- **about 2 tablespoons lemon juice**
- **375 g/12 oz skinned and boned cooked chicken, diced**
- **3 celery sticks, sliced thinly**
- **75 g/3 oz shelled walnuts, chopped roughly**
- **50 g/2 oz raisins**
- **2 Red Delicious apples**
- **salt and pepper**
- **crisp lettuce leaves, to serve**

1 Put the mayonnaise in a large bowl, add 2 tablespoons lemon juice and stir well to mix.
2 Add the chicken, celery, walnuts and raisins to the mayonnaise and stir well to mix.
3 Core and dice the apples, then add immediately to the salad and stir well to coat. Add salt and pepper to taste, and more lemon juice if liked.
4 Line a salad bowl with lettuce leaves and pile the salad in the centre. Serve at room temperature.

Serves 4
Preparation time: 20 minutes

Warm Chicken Liver Salad with Honey and Mustard Dressing

For convenience, you can use the ready-prepared salad leaves available from most large supermarkets.

- **25 g/1 oz butter**
- **250 g/8 oz chicken livers, cores removed, cut into bite-sized pieces**
- **250 g/8 oz mixed salad leaves (radicchio, frisée, oak leaf lettuce and rocket)**
- **salt and pepper**

DRESSING:

- **3 tablespoons extra-virgin olive oil**
- **1 tablespoon raspberry vinegar**
- **2 teaspoons clear honey**
- **1 teaspoon coarse grain mustard**
- **salt and pepper**

1 First make the dressing. Put all the ingredients in a large salad bowl with salt and pepper to taste. Whisk with a fork until evenly combined and thick, then adjust the seasoning to taste. Set aside.

2 Melt the butter in a frying pan over a moderate heat until foaming. Add the chicken livers and toss vigorously for 5–8 minutes until the livers are browned on the outside, but still tinged with pink in the centre. Season to taste with salt and pepper.

3 Quickly toss the salad leaves in the dressing, then divide between four serving plates. Spoon the chicken livers and cooking juices over the top. Serve immediately as a first course or light lunch, with hot bread.

Serves 4

Preparation time: 10 minutes

Cooking time: 5–8 minutes

Duck Breast Salad with Orange and Balsamic Vinegar

Slivers of warm duck breast and cool segments of fresh orange are served on a bed of rocket with a sweet and spicy dressing. The duck breasts roast quickly in the oven while the salad and dressing take only minutes to prepare, making this an easy dish for a special lunch.

- **2 boneless duck breasts**
- **2 oranges**
- **2 handfuls (50–75 g/2–3 oz) rocket**
- **salt and pepper**

DRESSING:

- **2 tablespoons virgin olive oil**
- **1 tablespoon balsamic vinegar**
- **1 garlic clove, crushed**
- **pinch of mustard powder**
- **pinch of sugar**

1 Put the duck breasts skin-side down on a board, cover with greaseproof paper and pound with a rolling pin to flatten them slightly.

2 Remove the paper and turn the breasts skin-side up. Score the skin diagonally or in a criss-cross pattern with a very sharp knife. Rub the skin all over with salt.

3 Put the duck breasts skin-side up on a rack in a roasting tin. Place in a preheated oven, 200°C (400°F), Gas Mark 6 for 15–20 minutes or until the duck is done to your liking (duck breasts are best served rare).

4 Meanwhile, peel and segment the oranges over a bowl to catch the juice. Set the segments aside. Put the dressing ingredients in the bowl with the orange juice, add salt and pepper to taste and stir well to mix. Reserve some whole rocket leaves for garnish and roughly chop the remainder.

5 When the duck breasts are cooked, transfer them to a board and slice them very thinly on the diagonal, removing the skin if preferred.

6 Place the chopped rocket leaves in the centre of individual plates and arrange the duck slices and orange segments on top. Spoon over the dressing and garnish with rocket leaves. Serve at room temperature.

Serves 2

Preparation time: 15 minutes

Cooking time: 15–20 minutes

Oven temperature: 200°C (400°F), Gas Mark 6

Chicken and Spinach Pinwheels

- 6 large boneless chicken breast portions, skinned
- salt and pepper
- basil sprigs, to garnish

FILLING:

- 250 g/8 oz fresh spinach leaves, washed
- 125 g/4 oz ricotta cheese
- ¼ teaspoon freshly grated nutmeg

TOMATO SAUCE:

- 2 tablespoons virgin olive oil
- 1 small onion, chopped finely
- 1 garlic clove, crushed
- 500 g/1 lb ripe tomatoes, peeled, deseeded and chopped roughly
- 1 tablespoon tomato purée
- 150 ml/¼ pint dry white wine
- good pinch of sugar
- 2 teaspoons chopped fresh basil

1 For the tomato sauce, heat the oil in a pan, add the onion and garlic and fry over a gentle heat, stirring, for 5 minutes or until softened.

2 Add the tomatoes and fry for 5 minutes, then add the tomato purée, wine, sugar and salt and pepper to taste. Bring to the boil, then lower the heat, cover and simmer, stirring occasionally, for 30 minutes.

3 Meanwhile, prepare the filling. Put the spinach in a large saucepan with only the water that clings to the leaves and a good pinch of salt. Cook over a gentle heat for 5 minutes or until wilted. Drain well and chop finely, then mix with the ricotta, nutmeg and salt and pepper to taste.

4 Prepare the chicken. Make a long horizontal slit through the thickness of each breast, without cutting right through. Open out the chicken and place between 2 sheets of greaseproof paper. Flatten each one by pounding with a rolling pin. Remove the paper.

5 Spread the filling over the chicken, leaving a 2.5 cm/1 inch border all around. Roll up each breast in a Swiss roll shape, tucking in the ends.

6 Put each roll on a piece of buttered or oiled foil, roll up tightly and twist the ends to enclose. Set aside.

7 Remove the tomato sauce from the heat and then add salt and pepper to taste. Set aside the tomato sauce whilst you cook the chicken.

8 Bring a wide shallow pan of water to the boil, add the chicken parcels in a single layer and poach over a gentle heat for 15 minutes.

9 Reheat the tomato sauce until hot. Meanwhile, remove the chicken parcels from the water with a slotted spoon, unwrap and slice thickly on the diagonal, using a sharp knife and a sawing action to make neat slices. Stir the basil into the tomato sauce, then taste the sauce for seasoning. Spoon the sauce on to warmed plates, arrange the chicken pinwheels on the sauce and garnish with basil sprigs. Serve immediately.

Serves 6

Preparation time: 30 minutes
Cooking time: about 45 minutes

Turkey Salad with Cranberry and Nut Dressing

This is the perfect recipe for using up leftovers. Hazelnuts are used here, but you can use any nut, with the corresponding nut oil.

- **about 375 g/12 oz skinned and boned cooked turkey, sliced thinly**
- **2 heads of chicory, quartered lengthways**
- **orange twists, to garnish (optional)**

DRESSING:

- **4 tablespoons hazelnut oil**
- **juice of 1 orange**
- **1 tablespoon raspberry vinegar or red wine vinegar**
- **1 tablespoon cranberry sauce or jelly**
- **50 g/2 oz shelled hazelnuts, chopped roughly**
- **salt and pepper**

1 First make the dressing. Put all the ingredients in a jug with salt and pepper to taste and whisk well to combine.

2 Arrange the turkey slices and chicory quarters on a serving platter in a circle, alternating them to make an attractive pattern.

3 Whisk the dressing again, then spoon over the turkey and chicory. Garnish with orange twists, if liked. Serve at room temperature.

Serves 4

Preparation time: 20 minutes

Chargrilled Chicken with Tomato-Chilli Salsa

Authentic chilli salsas hail from Mexico where they are always made fiery hot. Chillies vary enormously in their 'hotness', but generally the smaller they are the hotter they will be, so it is up to you to decide how hot you like your salsa.

- **2 large boneless chicken breast portions, skinned**
- **4 tablespoons virgin olive oil**
- **finely grated zest and juice of 2 limes**
- **salt and pepper**
- **fresh salad leaves, to serve**

TOMATO-CHILLI SALSA:

- **250 g/8 oz cherry tomatoes, quartered lengthways**
- **1–2 fresh red or green chillies, deseeded and diced very finely**
- **2 garlic cloves, crushed**
- **3 tablespoons extra-virgin olive oil**
- **juice of 1 lime**
- **2 tablespoons chopped fresh coriander**
- **½ teaspoon sugar**

TO GARNISH:

- **lime wedges**
- **coriander sprigs**

1 Put the chicken breasts on a board, cover with greaseproof paper and pound with a rolling pin to flatten slightly. Remove the paper and place the chicken in a shallow dish. Whisk together the olive oil, lime zest and juice and pepper to taste. Brush over the chicken, then cover and marinate at room temperature for about 1 hour.
2 To make the salsa, put all the ingredients in a bowl with salt and pepper to taste and stir well to mix. Cover and chill in the refrigerator until serving time.
3 Brush a little of the oil from the chicken on a ridged cast iron pan and place over a moderate heat until hot. Put the chicken breasts and remaining oil on the pan and cook for 3–5 minutes on each side or until the chicken feels tender when pierced with a skewer or fork.
4 Serve the chicken on a bed of salad leaves, garnished with lime wedges and coriander sprigs. Serve the salsa alongside.

Serves 2
Preparation time: 15 minutes, plus marinating
Cooking time: 6–10 minutes

VARIATION

Duck with Pineapple Salsa

1 Put 2 boneless duck breasts skin-side down on a board, cover with greaseproof paper and pound with a rolling pin to flatten. Remove the paper and score the skin with a very sharp knife. Place the duck skin-side up in a shallow dish.
2 Drain 1 x 220 g/8 oz can pineapple slices in natural juice. Mix the juice with 2 tablespoons virgin olive oil and season to taste. Pour over the duck, cover and marinate for 1 hour.
3 Make the pineapple salsa. Finely chop the pineapple and then mix with 2 fresh red chillies, deseeded and finely chopped, 1 garlic clove, crushed, 1 tablespoon extra-virgin olive oil, ½ teaspoon sugar and seasoning. Stir to mix, cover and chill.
4 Brush a ridged cast iron pan with oil and place over a moderate heat until hot. Add the duck skin-side down and cook for 5 minutes, pressing down firmly to flatten the breasts.
5 Drain off the fat and turn the duck over. Cook for a further 7–8 minutes or until tender. Remove and slice very thinly on the diagonal, removing and discarding the skin if preferred. Serve as in the main recipe.

Serves 2
Preparation time: 15 minutes, plus marinating
Cooking time: 12–13 minutes

Family Meals

French Roast Chicken

1 x 2 kg/4 lb oven-ready, corn-fed chicken, giblets removed
1 bunch of fresh mixed herbs (such as tarragon, parsley, rosemary, thyme)
1 garlic clove, quartered
75 g/3 oz butter
300 ml/½ pint hot Giblet Stock (see page 9)
125 ml/4 fl oz dry white wine
salt and pepper

1 Wash and dry the chicken cavity, insert the herbs and garlic and season. Truss the chicken, spread it with butter and sprinkle with pepper. Place on its side in a close-fitting roasting tin. Pour half the stock around it. Roast in a preheated oven, 200°C (400°F), Gas Mark 6, for 1 hour 40 minutes or until tender. Turn over every 25 minutes, first on its breast, then on its other side, and finally on its back. Baste well each time it is turned.
2 Remove the chicken, cover with foil and set aside to rest in a warm place.
3 Pour off most of the fat, set the tin on top of the stove and add the wine and remaining stock. Bring to the boil, scraping the sediment from the tin. Simmer, stirring, until the sauce is reduced and thickened. Check the seasoning.
4 Carve the chicken and place on warmed plates with the sauce. Serve with garlic 'flowers' – allow 1 garlic head each. Slice off the tops, place cut-side up in an oiled ovenproof dish and drizzle 1 tablespoon olive oil over each. Cook for the last 50 minutes of roasting time; baste after 25 minutes. To eat, squeeze out the garlic flesh.

Serves 4
Preparation time: 20 minutes
Cooking time: 1 hour 40 minutes
Oven temperature: 200°C (400°F), Gas Mark 6

Turkey Schnitzels

These are a variation of Wiener schnitzels, veal escalopes shallow fried in an egg and breadcrumb coating. Thin and crispy, they are very more-ish, so always make more than one per person, to cater for second helpings.

- **6 thick slices of very stale white bread (at least 2 days old), crusts removed**
- **6 turkey escalopes**
- **3 tablespoons plain flour**
- **1 egg, beaten**
- **about 6 tablespoons rapeseed oil**
- **salt and pepper**

TO SERVE:

- **lemon wedges**
- **parsley sprigs**

1 Grate the stale bread into very fine crumbs, using the finest drum of a Mouli grater, or the finest grid of a box grater. (Do not use a food processor or blender because it will not work the crumbs fine enough.)
2 Put the turkey escalopes between 2 sheets of greaseproof paper and flatten them by pounding them with a rolling pin. Remove the paper. If the escalopes are large, cut them into serving portions according to how you like them.
3 Season both sides of each piece of turkey with salt and pepper to taste. Spread the flour out on a plate in front of you. Spread the beaten egg out on a second plate and the breadcrumbs out on a third.
4 Coat the turkey first in the flour, then in the beaten egg, and then in the breadcrumbs. Press the breadcrumbs on firmly so that they adhere. Chill, uncovered, in the refrigerator for at least 30 minutes.
5 Heat 3 tablespoons of the oil in a large frying pan (preferably non-stick) until very hot but not smoking. Add as many schnitzels as will fit comfortably in the pan and fry over a high heat for 3 minutes on each side or until the crumbs are golden brown and the turkey feels tender when pierced with a skewer or fork. Remove with a fish slice and drain on paper towels.
6 Repeat with more oil and schnitzels, wiping the frying pan clean between each batch or the schnitzel coating will be too dark. Serve hot, with lemon wedges and parsley sprigs.

Serves 4
Preparation time: 30 minutes, plus chilling
Cooking time: 6 minutes each batch

Oven-fried Chicken Drumsticks

These drumsticks are cooked in the oven without fat, making them a healthy alternative to the more traditional fried chicken, and egg whites are used rather than whole eggs for the coating, to help further reduce fat and cholesterol. The cayenne pepper gives the coating a spicy taste, but you may prefer to leave it out if you are cooking these for young children.

- **8 chicken drumsticks, skinned**
- **2 tablespoons plain flour**
- **¼ teaspoon cayenne pepper**
- **2 egg whites, whisked lightly**
- **75 g/3 oz fresh breadcrumbs (white or wholemeal according to taste)**
- **2 tablespoons chopped fresh herbs (e.g. parsley, chives, tarragon, rosemary)**
- **2 tablespoons rapeseed oil**
- **salt and pepper**
- **lemon wedges, to serve**

1 Season the chicken drumsticks with salt and pepper to taste. Spread the flour out on a plate in front of you, add the cayenne pepper and stir well to mix. Spread the whisked egg whites out on a second plate and the breadcrumbs out on a third. Mix the herbs with the breadcrumbs.
2 Coat the chicken drumsticks first in the flour, then in the whisked egg whites, and then in the breadcrumbs. Press the breadcrumbs on firmly so that they adhere.
3 Heat the oil in a large frying pan (preferably non-stick) until very hot but not smoking. Add the drumsticks and fry over a moderate heat, turning frequently, for about 5 minutes until golden on all sides.
4 Transfer the drumsticks to a baking tray and place in a preheated oven, 190°C (375°F), Gas Mark 5 for 40 minutes or until the chicken feels tender when pierced with a skewer or fork. Turn the drumsticks over from time to time to ensure that they brown evenly. Serve hot, with lemon wedges. Jacket potatoes or new potatoes and a seasonal vegetable or salad would be appropriate low-fat accompaniments.

Serves 4
Preparation time: 15 minutes
Cooking time: about 45 minutes
Oven temperature: 190°C (375°F), Gas Mark 5

St Clement's Chicken

- 6 part-boned chicken breasts
- 3 tablespoons rapeseed oil
- 1 tablespoon plain flour
- 250 ml/8 fl oz unsweetened orange juice
- 250 ml/8 fl oz hot Chicken Stock (see pages 8–9)
- finely grated zest and juice of 1 lemon
- 2 teaspoons finely chopped fresh sage
- salt and pepper

TO GARNISH:

- ½ orange, cut into 6 slices
- ½ lemon, cut into 6 slices
- a handful of sage leaves

1 Sauté the chicken breasts in the oil for about 10 minutes until golden. Remove with a slotted spoon and set aside on a plate.

2 Sprinkle in the flour and cook, stirring, for 1–2 minutes. Blend in the orange juice, stirring, then add the stock together with the lemon zest and juice. Bring to the boil, stirring, then lower the heat and add the sage, and salt and pepper to taste.

3 Return the chicken and its juices to the pan, cover and simmer for 20 minutes until tender. Turn and baste during this time. Check seasoning.

4 Serve hot, garnished with orange and lemon slices and sage leaves.

Serves 6

Preparation time: 5–10 minutes

Cooking time: about 30 minutes

Chow Mein

- 2 tablespoons rapeseed oil
- 4 spring onions or 1 onion, sliced thinly
- 2.5 cm/1 inch piece of fresh root ginger, crushed
- 1 garlic clove, crushed
- 250 g/8 oz skinless chicken breast fillets, cut diagonally into thin strips
- 1 x 250 g/8 oz packet Chinese egg noodles
- 125 g/4 oz mangetout, topped and tailed, cut crossways if large
- 125 g/4 oz boiled ham, cut into thin strips
- 2-3 tablespoons soy sauce, to taste
- 2 tablespoons rice wine or dry sherry
- 2 teaspoons sesame oil
- 1 teaspoon sugar
- salt and pepper

1 Heat a wok or large deep frying pan over a moderate heat until hot. Add the oil and heat until hot but not smoking. Add the spring onions or onion, ginger and garlic and stir-fry over a gentle heat for 1–2 minutes until softened but not coloured.

2 Add the strips of chicken breast and stir-fry over a moderate heat for 3–4 minutes until they change colour on all sides.

3 Meanwhile, put the egg noodles in a large bowl and cover with boiling water. Leave to stand.

4 Add the mangetout to the chicken in the wok and stir-fry for about 2–3 minutes or until the chicken is tender when pierced with a fork.

5 Drain the noodles, add to the wok with the strips of ham, and toss over a high heat until hot. Add the soy sauce, rice wine or sherry, sesame oil, sugar and seasoning to taste. Toss until all the ingredients are hot and glistening. Serve immediately.

Serves 3–4

Preparation time: 20 minutes

Cooking time: about 10 minutes

Chicken Pot Pie

- **750 g/1½ lb old potatoes**
- **50 g/2 oz butter**
- **40 g/1½ oz plain flour**
- **600 ml/1 pint milk**
- **2 tablespoons finely chopped fresh parsley, plus a little extra to garnish**
- **¼ teaspoon mustard powder**
- **375 g/12 oz skinned and boned cooked chicken, cut into bite-sized pieces**
- **200 g/7 oz frozen mixed vegetables, thawed**
- **3 hard-boiled eggs, shelled and sliced**
- **a little melted butter**
- **50 g/2 oz grated cheese, such as Double Gloucester or Red Leicester**
- **salt and pepper**

1 Boil the potatoes until just tender. Drain and slice into thin rounds.
2 Make a white sauce with the butter, flour and milk. Add 2 tablespoons of the chopped parsley and the mustard powder and stir in the chicken and mixed vegetables. Season to taste.
3 Pour the mixture into a dish and arrange the hard-boiled eggs on top, then add the potato rounds. Brush with melted butter and sprinkle with the cheese. Cook the pie in a preheated oven, 190°C (375°F), Gas Mark 5 for 30 minutes or until golden. Garnish with the parsley.

Serves 4
Preparation time: 30 minutes
Cooking time: 30 minutes
Oven temperature: 190°C (375°F), Gas Mark 5

Old English Chicken Pie

- 2 tablespoons rapeseed oil
- 12 skinned and boned chicken thighs, cut into small bite-sized pieces
- 15 g/½ oz butter
- 375 g/12 oz carrots, sliced thickly
- 375 g/12 oz turnips or parsnips, sliced thickly
- 2 leeks, trimmed, cleaned and sliced thickly
- 2 tablespoons plain flour
- ½ teaspoon ground mixed spice
- 300 ml/½ pint dry cider
- 150 ml/¼ pint hot Chicken Stock (see pages 8–9)
- 250 g/8 oz puff pastry, thawed if frozen
- beaten egg, to glaze
- salt and pepper

1 Heat the oil in a flameproof casserole. Sauté the chicken over a moderate heat for about 5 minutes until coloured on all sides. Remove and set aside on a plate.
2 Melt the butter in the casserole, then add the vegetables and toss to coat in the oil and butter. Lower the heat, cover and sweat gently for 10 minutes.
3 Sprinkle in the flour and mixed spice. Cook, stirring, for 1–2 minutes, then gradually stir in the cider and stock. Bring to the boil, stirring, season to taste, and add the chicken with any juices from the plate. Cover and cook over a gentle heat for about 10 minutes. Turn into a bowl and leave until cold.

4 Roll out the pastry on a lightly floured surface and cut out a lid to fit a 1 litre/2 pint pie dish. Cut out a strip of pastry to go around the rim of the dish. From the trimmings, cut out pastry leaves for the top of the pie.
5 Spoon the cold mixture into the pie dish, putting a pie funnel in the centre. Brush the rim of the dish with water. Press the pastry strip into place, brush with water, and put the lid on top. Cut a hole for the funnel.
6 Press the edges to seal, knock up and flute. Brush the pastry with beaten egg and stick the pastry leaves on top. Brush again with beaten egg.
7 Place in a preheated oven, 220°C (425°F), Gas Mark 7 for 30 minutes or until the pastry is golden. Serve hot, straight from the dish, with a fresh vegetable and mashed potatoes.

Serves 4
Preparation time: 45 minutes, plus cooling
Cooking time: 30 minutes
Oven temperature: 220°C (425°F), Gas Mark 7

Chicken Cannelloni

- **50 g/2 oz frozen sweetcorn kernels**
- **50 g/2 oz butter**
- **50 g/2 oz plain flour**
- **700 ml/24 fl oz milk**
- **175 g/6 oz Cheddar cheese, grated**
- **250 g/8 oz skinned and boned cooked chicken, shredded**
- **¼ teaspoon freshly grated nutmeg**
- **12 cannelloni tubes**
- **good pinch of paprika**
- **salt and pepper**

1 Cook the frozen sweetcorn kernels in salted boiling water for 3 minutes, or according to packet instructions, until tender. Drain well and set aside.
2 Melt the butter in a saucepan, sprinkle in the flour and stir over a moderate heat for 1–2 minutes. Remove from the heat and add half the milk a little at a time, beating vigorously after each addition.
3 Return the pan to the heat and bring to the boil, stirring all the time. Lower the heat and simmer, stirring, for about 5 minutes until very thick and smooth. Remove the pan from the heat and transfer half the sauce to a bowl.
4 Add one-third of the grated Cheddar to the sauce in the bowl with the chicken, sweetcorn, half the nutmeg, and salt and pepper to taste. Stir well.
5 Over a moderate heat, gradually beat the remaining milk into the sauce in the pan, bring to the boil and simmer, stirring, for 5 minutes until thick and smooth. Add half the remaining cheese, the remaining nutmeg, and salt and pepper to taste. Stir until the cheese melts. Remove the from the heat, then pour about one-third of the sauce into a large ovenproof dish. Spread evenly.
6 With a teaspoon, fill the cannelloni tubes with the chicken mixture. Place the tubes in a single layer in the dish as you fill them.
7 Pour over the remaining sauce and sprinkle with the remaining cheese and the paprika. Place in a preheated oven, 190°C (375°F), Gas Mark 5 for 30–35 minutes until bubbling and golden. Serve hot, with a mixed salad.

Serves 4–6
Preparation time: 30 minutes
Cooking time: 30–35 minutes
Oven temperature: 190°C (375°F), Gas Mark 5

VARIATION

Chicken Pasticciata

Another good pasta recipe. This one, smooth and creamy, is popular with children.

1 Cook 175 g/6 oz penne or other pasta shapes, until al dente. Make a white sauce with 25 g/1 oz each of butter and flour and 600 ml/1 pint milk. Remove from the heat and add 125 g/4 oz mozzarella, diced, 20 g/¾ oz grated Parmesan, a pinch of nutmeg, salt and pepper.
2 Drain the pasta well and mix with 250 g/8 oz skinned and boned cooked chicken, cut into thin strips. Mix with two-thirds of the cheese sauce.
3 Tip the mixture into a baking dish and spread it out. Mix 2 beaten eggs into the remaining sauce and pour over the top. Sprinkle with 20 g/¾ oz grated Parmesan and bake in a preheated oven, 190°C (375°F), Gas Mark 5 for 20 minutes or until bubbling and golden. Serve with a crunchy salad.

Serves 4
Preparation time: 30 minutes
Cooking time: 20 minutes
Oven temperature: 190°C (375°F), Gas Mark 5

Chicken Liver Risotto

In a genuine Italian risotto, the liquid is added a little at a time, which means that the cook must stand over the pot for the entire cooking time. This recipe cheats a little, but it is much more convenient and less time-consuming – and it works very well.

- **2 tablespoons virgin olive oil**
- **1 onion, chopped finely**
- **250 g/8 oz chicken livers, cores removed, chopped roughly**
- **1 garlic clove, crushed**
- **300 g/10 oz Italian risotto rice**
- **125 ml/4 fl oz dry white wine**
- **about 1 litre/1¾ pints hot Chicken Stock (see pages 8–9)**
- **large pinch of saffron threads**
- **125 g/4 oz frozen peas or petits pois**
- **salt and pepper**

TO FINISH:

- **6 tablespoons double cream**
- **2 tablespoons chopped fresh flat leaf parsley (optional)**
- **about 50 g/2 oz Parmesan cheese**

1 Heat the oil in a large flameproof casserole, add the onion and fry over a gentle heat, stirring frequently, for about 5 minutes until softened but not coloured.

2 Add the chicken livers and the crushed garlic, increase the heat to moderate and fry, stirring constantly, for 2–3 minutes or until the livers change colour on all sides.

3 Add the rice, stir well, then add the white wine and gently stir until the bubbles subside.

4 Pour in 600 ml/1 pint of the hot stock, add the saffron and salt and pepper to taste and stir well. Bring to the boil, then cover and simmer over a gentle heat for 10 minutes, stirring occasionally to prevent the rice from sticking to the bottom of the pan.

5 Add a further 400 ml/14 fl oz hot stock to the risotto, stir well to combine, then add the peas. Cover and simmer for a further 10 minutes, stirring occasionally and adding a little more stock if necessary.

6 Remove the pan from the heat and fold in the cream and the parsley, if using. Adjust the seasoning to taste. Serve hot, topped with shavings of Parmesan. A crisp green salad is the only accompaniment needed for this hearty lunch or supper dish.

Serves 4

Preparation time: 15–20 minutes

Cooking time: 20 minutes

Spiced Turkey Meatballs

If you like, you can form the minced turkey mixture into burger shapes and serve them in warmed buns with salad, in which case you should omit the sauce.

- **500 g/1 lb minced turkey**
- **1 small onion, chopped roughly**
- **1 garlic clove, chopped roughly**
- **50 g/2 oz crustless granary or wholemeal bread, torn into pieces**
- **finely grated zest of 1 lemon**
- **½ teaspoon ground allspice**
- **½ teaspoon ground cinnamon**
- **2 tablespoons rapeseed oil**
- **15 g/½ oz butter**
- **salt and pepper**
- **snipped chives, to garnish**

SAUCE:

- **125 ml/4 fl oz dry white wine**
- **4 tablespoons lemon juice**
- **4 tablespoons soured or double cream (optional)**

1 Put the minced turkey in a food processor with the onion, garlic, bread, lemon zest, allspice, cinnamon and salt and pepper to taste. Work until the ingredients are all finely and evenly mixed.

2 Turn the mixture out of the machine. With wet hands, shape the mixture into 24 ovals.

3 Heat the oil and butter in a large flameproof casserole or frying pan. Add half the meatballs and fry over a moderate heat for about 6 minutes, shaking the casserole or pan constantly, until browned on each side. Remove with a slotted spoon and drain on paper towels. Repeat with the remaining meatballs.

4 Make the sauce. Pour the wine and lemon juice into the casserole and stir to dissolve the pan juices. Bring to the boil, stirring, and boil until reduced slightly, then remove from the heat and stir in the soured or double cream, if using.

5 Transfer the meatballs to a warmed serving dish, pour over the sauce and sprinkle with snipped chives. Serve immediately, with buttered rice and a medley of colourful vegetables, such as broccoli or French beans and carrot juliennes.

Serves 4–6

Preparation time: 30 minutes

Cooking time: about 6 minutes each batch

Chicken and Sweetcorn Chowder

Rich and creamy, this American-style soup is substantial enough to serve as a main course with crusty bread. The cream added at the end is not essential if you prefer a dish that is less rich. Take care when adding salt as the bacon may be salty, especially if it is smoked.

- **1 tablespoon rapeseed oil**
- **125 g/4 oz streaky bacon rashers, rinds removed, chopped**
- **1 large onion, chopped finely**
- **500 g/1 lb potatoes, diced**
- **½ teaspoon dried mixed herbs**
- **600 ml/1 pint milk**
- **450 ml/¾ pint water**
- **1 bay leaf**
- **250–375 g/8–12 oz skinned and boned cooked chicken, diced**
- **1 x 325 g/11 oz can sweetcorn and peppers, drained**
- **150 ml/¼ pint single cream (optional)**
- **salt and pepper**
- **finely chopped fresh flat leaf parsley, to garnish**

1 Heat the oil in a large saucepan or flameproof casserole, add the chopped bacon and fry over a moderate heat for about 5 minutes until crispy. Remove the bacon with a slotted spoon and drain on paper towels. Chop or crumble the crispy bacon into pieces.

2 Add the onion to the pan and fry over a gentle heat, stirring frequently, for about 5 minutes until softened but not coloured. Add the diced potatoes and mixed herbs and stir to mix with the onion, then add the milk, water, bay leaf, and salt and pepper to taste.

3 Bring to the boil over a high heat, stirring, then lower the heat to moderate. Cover and simmer, stirring occasionally, for 20 minutes or until the potatoes are tender when pierced with a fork. Discard the bay leaf.

4 Add the chicken and sweetcorn and peppers. Heat through for about 5 minutes, then lower the heat and stir in the cream, if using. Adjust the seasoning to taste. Serve hot, sprinkled with the chopped crispy bacon and chopped parsley.

Serves 4

Preparation time: 20 minutes

Cooking time: about 30 minutes

VARIATION

Turkey and Chestnut Soup

Another delicious soup recipe, and an excellent way to use up leftover Christmas turkey.

1 Break the turkey carcass into pieces and place in a large saucepan with any leftover stuffing, 1 onion, 1 carrot and 1 celery stick, all chopped, 2 sprigs of thyme and salt and pepper. Add 1.8 litres/3 pints water and bring to the boil. Cover and simmer for 3 hours. Add extra water when necessary.

2 Remove the carcass and vegetables and discard. Strain the stock and add any leftover turkey meat cut into bite-sized pieces. Heat 2 tablespoons oil in the rinsed-out pan. Add 2 large potatoes, 1 onion, 1 carrot and 1 celery stick, all chopped. Cook gently, stirring, for 5 minutes, pour in the strained stock and bring to the boil. Reduce the heat and simmer for 20 minutes, then add 1 x 475 g/15 oz can whole chestnuts in brine, drained, and 3 tablespoons sherry or port. Reheat, check seasoning and serve hot, garnished with thyme.

Serves 6

Preparation time: 20 minutes

Cooking time: 3½ hours

Chicken Tzatziki

Sizzling hot chicken is served with a cool and refreshing yogurt, cucumber and mint salad. The combination of fresh and dried mint intensifies the minty flavour.

- **4 chicken portions or 8 chicken thighs**
- **2 x 150 g/5 oz cartons Greek-style yogurt**
- **3 tablespoons virgin olive oil**
- **2 garlic cloves, crushed**
- **2 teaspoons dried mint**
- **½ cucumber, peeled and chopped finely**
- **2 tablespoons finely chopped fresh mint**
- **salt and pepper**

TO GARNISH (OPTIONAL):

- **cucumber slices**
- **fresh mint sprigs**

1 Score the the chicken pieces deeply with a sharp knife, cutting right down as far as the bone.
2 Mix together half the yogurt with 2 tablespoons of the oil, half the garlic and dried mint and pepper to taste. Put the chicken in a shallow dish and spoon or brush the yogurt mixture over all the pieces. Cover and marinate in the refrigerator for at least 4 hours, preferably overnight.
3 Put the chicken on the grid over hot charcoal on the barbecue. Cook, turning frequently, for about 20 minutes until the chicken is charred on the outside and no longer pink on the inside. Alternatively, cook under a hot grill, turning frequently, for about 20 minutes.
4 Meanwhile, put the remaining yogurt, garlic and dried mint in a bowl and stir well to mix. Add the cucumber, fresh mint and salt and pepper to taste and stir again. Turn into a serving bowl, drizzle with the remaining oil and garnish with cucumber slices and mint sprigs, if using.
5 Serve the chicken hot, with the tzatziki salad. Hot pitta bread and a tomato salad make good accompaniments.

Serves 4
Preparation time: 15 minutes, plus marinating
Cooking time: about 20 minutes

VARIATION

Sweet and Sour Chicken Drumsticks

1 Score 8 chicken drumsticks deeply with a sharp knife, cutting right down as far as the bone.
2 In a bowl mix together 4 tablespoons tomato ketchup, 2 tablespoons wine vinegar, 2 tablespoons Worcestershire sauce, 2 tablespoons runny honey, and 2 tablespoons soft brown sugar. Put the drumsticks in a shallow dish and brush the sweet and sour mixture all over them. Cover and marinate in the refrigerator for at least 4 hours, preferably overnight.
3 Put the drumsticks on the grid over hot charcoal on the barbecue. Cook, turning frequently, for 20 minutes or until the chicken is charred on the outside and no longer pink on the inside. Serve hot or cold.

Serves 4
Preparation time: 15 minutes, plus marinating
Cooking time: about 20 minutes

Around the World

Cajun Chicken

125 g/4 oz unsalted butter
6 large boneless chicken breast portions, skinned
50 black peppercorns
10 allspice berries
1 tablespoon cayenne pepper
2 teaspoons garlic salt
lemon wedges, to serve

1 Melt the butter in a saucepan, pour into a bowl and leave to cool.
2 With a sharp knife, score the chicken breasts diagonally in several places. In a mortar and pestle, coarsely crush the peppercorns and allspice, then add the cayenne and garlic salt.
3 Rub the spice mixture over the chicken, working it into the slashes in the flesh. Put the chicken in a single layer in a dish and spoon the cooled melted butter over it. Cover and chill in the refrigerator for 2 hours.
4 Heat a ridged cast iron pan over a moderate heat until hot. Add the chicken pieces and cook for 15–20 minutes, turning once, until charred and tender. Serve hot, with lemon wedges. For a typical Cajun accompaniment, serve with rice mixed with finely chopped green pepper, celery, spring onions and garlic, flavoured with black pepper, cayenne and paprika.

Serves 6
Preparation time: 15 minutes, plus chilling
Cooking time: 15–20 minutes

Jambalaya

Mussels replace the traditional oysters in this Creole dish from New Orleans. Creole cooking is a mixture of French, Spanish and South American influences.

- **500 g/1 lb fresh mussels**
- **150 ml/¼ pint dry white wine**
- **150 ml/¼ pint water**
- **1 bouquet garni**
- **2 garlic cloves, crushed**
- **1 x 1.5 kg/3 lb oven ready chicken, giblets removed, cut into 8 pieces**
- **175 g/6 oz chorizo sausage, chopped**
- **2 tablespoons rapeseed oil**
- **2 onions, chopped finely**
- **2 celery sticks, chopped finely**
- **1 green pepper, cored, deseeded and chopped**
- **1 red pepper, cored, deseeded and chopped**
- **1 x 425 g/14 oz can chopped tomatoes**
- **1 teaspoon dried thyme**
- **1 teaspoon dried oregano**
- **1 teaspoon cayenne pepper**
- **about 600 ml/1 pint hot Chicken Stock (see pages 8–9) or water**
- **500 g/1 lb long-grain rice**
- **2 bay leaves, broken up**
- **salt and pepper**

1 Scrub the mussels with a stiff brush and scrape off the beards and barnacles with a small, sharp knife. Discard any open mussels.
2 Put the wine, water, bouquet garni, garlic, mussels and salt and pepper in a large saucepan. Cover tightly with a lid and bring to the boil. Shake the pan and simmer for 5 minutes or until the mussels open. Remove them from the liquid and set aside, discarding any which remain closed. Strain the cooking liquid and reserve.
3 Fry the chicken and chorizo in the oil in a large flameproof casserole, stirring frequently, for 5 minutes. Remove with a slotted spoon and set aside on a plate.
4 Add the onions, celery and peppers to the casserole and fry, stirring constantly, for 5 minutes until softened. Add the tomatoes, thyme, oregano and cayenne and stir. Add the mussel cooking liquid and the stock or water. Bring to the boil, stirring. Add the rice and bay leaves and salt and pepper to taste, then stir well to mix.
5 Return the chicken and chorizo and their juices to the casserole, cover and simmer for 40 minutes or until the chicken is tender and the rice al dente. Add more stock as needed. Discard the bay leaves.
6 Place the mussels on top of the chicken and rice, cover tightly and heat through for a further 5 minutes. Serve straight from the casserole.

Serves 6
Preparation time: 40 minutes
Cooking time: about 1 hour

Chicken and Smoked Ham Gumbo

Gumbo is a kind of soupy stew from Louisiana, usually made with seafood, such as shrimps, crab and scallops. Here it is made with chicken and smoked ham, which is equally delicious. As a variation, you can substitute 375 g/12 oz peeled prawns or 8 scallops for the ham and cook them for just a few minutes.

- **5 tablespoons rapeseed oil**
- **40 g/1½ oz plain flour**
- **1 large onion, chopped finely**
- **1 red pepper, cored, deseeded and chopped finely**
- **2 garlic cloves, crushed**
- **1.2 litres/2 pints hot Chicken Stock (see pages 8–9)**
- **1 x 425 g/14 oz can chopped or crushed tomatoes**
- **2 tablespoons chopped fresh parsley**
- **1 tablespoon chopped fresh thyme**
- **¼ teaspoon cayenne pepper**
- **750 g/1½ lb skinned and boned chicken thighs, cut into bite-sized pieces**
- **250 g/8 oz okra, sliced thinly**
- **250 g/8 oz smoked ham in one piece, cut into bite-sized pieces**
- **salt and pepper**
- **chopped spring onions or tiny sprigs of thyme, to garnish (optional)**

1 Heat the oil in a large flameproof casserole, sprinkle in the flour and stir well to form a roux. Cook the roux, stirring constantly, over a very gentle heat for 10–15 minutes or until a rich, nutty brown in colour.
2 Add the onion, red pepper and garlic and fry, stirring frequently, for about 5 minutes until softened.
3 Gradually stir in the stock, then add the tomatoes, herbs, cayenne and salt and pepper to taste. Increase the heat and bring to the boil, stirring.
4 Lower the heat and add the chicken. Cover and simmer over a gentle heat, stirring occasionally, for 40 minutes or until the chicken is tender when pierced with a fork. Add the okra and smoked ham for the last 10 minutes of cooking.
5 Adjust the seasoning to taste and serve hot, garnished with spring onions or thyme, if using. Gumbo is traditionally served over boiled rice in soup plates.

Serves 6
Preparation time: 40 minutes
Cooking time: about 1 hour

Jamaican Jerk Chicken

Jerk pork is one of Jamaica's most famous national dishes. It is cooked over hot coals at roadside stands all over the island. Here, chicken drumsticks are 'jerked' instead of pork, making perfect outdoor food to eat with your fingers. In winter, it can be cooked under the grill.

- **2 tablespoons rapeseed oil**
- **1 small onion, chopped finely**
- **10 allspice berries**
- **2 red hot chillies, deseeded and chopped roughly**
- **juice of 1 lime**
- **1 teaspoon salt**
- **12 chicken drumsticks**

1 Put all of the ingredients, except the chicken drumsticks, in a food processor or spice mill and grind to a paste.
2 Score the chicken drumsticks deeply with a sharp pointed knife, cutting right down as far as the bone.
3 Coat the chicken with the jerk seasoning mixture, brushing it into the slashes in the meat so that the flavour will penetrate. Cover and marinate in the refrigerator overnight.
4 Put the drumsticks on the grid over hot charcoal on the barbecue. Cook, turning frequently, for about 20 minutes until the chicken is charred on the outside and no longer pink on the inside. Serve hot, warm or cold, with ice-cold beer.

Serves 4–6
Preparation time: 15 minutes, plus marinating
Cooking time: about 20 minutes

VARIATION

Silver Sands Chicken

1 Replace the drumsticks with a whole 2 kg/4 lb oven-ready chicken, giblets removed, and score the flesh deeply all over.
2 Make the following jerk seasoning: stir together ½ small onion, grated, 2 garlic cloves, crushed, 1 tablespoon ground allspice, 2 teaspoons coarsely ground black pepper, ½ teaspoon dried thyme, ¼ teaspoon each grated nutmeg, ground cinnamon and salt.
3 Coat the chicken with the seasoning and marinate it as for the drumsticks in the main recipe.
4 Cook the whole chicken, on a rack in a kettle barbecue, turning it frequently, for 1¼ hours or until the juices run clear when the thickest part of a thigh is pierced with a skewer or fork. Cut the chicken into pieces to serve.

Serves 4–6
Preparation time: 15 minutes, plus marinating
Cooking time: 1¼–1½ hours

Thai Curry

If you cannot obtain kapi, use 2 tablespoons fish sauce instead.

- **1 fresh coconut**
- **1.2 litres/2 pints boiling water**
- **2 large garlic cloves, chopped roughly**
- **5 cm/2 inch piece of fresh root ginger, chopped roughly**
- **3 small fresh red or green chillies, deseeded and chopped roughly**
- **1 stem of lemon grass, lower part only, sliced**
- **6 sprigs fresh coriander**
- **5 mm/¼ inch slice of Thai dried shrimp paste (kapi)**
- **2 teaspoons turmeric**
- **seeds of 6 cardamom pods**
- **1 teaspoon coriander seeds**
- **1 teaspoon cumin seeds**
- **½ teaspoon ground mace**
- **1 kg/2 lb skinned and boned chicken thighs, cut into bite-sized pieces**
- **1 tablespoon fish sauce (nam pla)**
- **salt**

1 First make the coconut milk. Pierce 2 holes in the eyes of the coconut and drain off the liquid from the centre. Crack the coconut open with a hammer, then dig the flesh out of the shell.

2 Put the coconut flesh in a food processor and chop finely. Add the boiling water and process for about 30 seconds.

3 Tip the coconut and liquid into a muslin-lined sieve set over a bowl, and let the coconut 'milk' drain through, pressing firmly with the back of a metal spoon to extract as much of the liquid as possible.

4 Put the garlic, ginger, chillies and lemon grass in the food processor. Remove the coriander leaves from the stems and reserve. Put the coriander stems, shrimp paste, turmeric, cardamom, coriander and cumin seeds and the mace in the food processor, with a few spoonfuls of coconut milk. Work to a paste.

5 Heat a wok or large frying pan until hot. Spoon the thick 'cream' off the surface of the coconut milk and put it in the wok. Add the spice paste and stir-fry over a moderate heat for a few minutes until the oil separates, then continue stir-frying the spices in the oil until the mixture gives off a rich aroma and is quite dry.

6 Add the chicken and stir to coat in the spice mixture, then pour in the remaining coconut milk. Add the fish sauce and cook, stirring frequently, for 40 minutes or until the chicken is tender when pierced with a skewer or fork. Taste and add salt if necessary.

7 Transfer the curry to a warmed dish and scatter the reserved coriander over the surface. Serve hot, with plain steamed or boiled rice.

Serves 4–6

Preparation time: 20 minutes

Cooking time: about 45 minutes

Indonesian Chicken and Coconut Curry

- **1 small onion, chopped roughly**
- **5 cm/2 inch piece of fresh root ginger, chopped roughly**
- **2 garlic cloves, chopped roughly**
- **1 fresh green or red chilli, deseeded and chopped roughly**
- **2 stems of lemon grass, lower part only, sliced**
- **2 tablespoons rapeseed oil**
- **1 teaspoon turmeric**
- **1 kg/2 lb skinned and boned chicken thighs, cut into bite-sized pieces**
- **250 ml/8 fl oz canned coconut milk**
- **150 ml/¼ pint water**
- **salt**

TO FINISH:

- **50 g/2 oz natural unsalted cashews or macadamia nuts**
- **50 g/2 oz desiccated coconut**

1 Crush the onion, ginger, garlic, chilli and lemon grass to a paste.
2 Heat a wok or large deep frying pan until hot. Add the oil and warm over a moderate heat until hot but not smoking. Add the chilli paste and stir-fry over a gentle heat for 1–2 minutes until fragrant.
3 Add the turmeric and stir-fry for 1–2 minutes, then add the chicken, coconut milk and water and bring to the boil. Stir well, then lower the heat. Cover and simmer gently, stirring frequently, for 40 minutes or until the chicken is tender.
4 Meanwhile, finely chop the cashews or macadamia nuts, or pound them in a mortar and pestle, then place them in a small heavy-botttomed frying pan along with the desiccated coconut. Dry-fry over a gentle heat for a few minutes, stirring and tossing the mixture until it is toasted to a rich, nutty brown.
5 When the chicken is tender and the sauce has become rich and thick, add salt to taste, then turn the curry into a warmed serving bowl. Sprinkle the toasted nut and coconut mixture over the top and serve the curry piping hot. Either plain boiled or steamed white rice is the perfect foil for such a rich dish.

Serves 4–6
Preparation time: 30 minutes
Cooking time: about 45 minutes

Chicken Satay

This Indonesian dish is best cooked over charcoal, but you can cook it under a hot grill if more convenient. Take care not to overcook the chicken.

- **4 large boneless chicken breast portions, skinned and cut diagonally into thin strips**

MARINADE:

- **¼ onion, grated or chopped very finely**
- **1 garlic clove, crushed**
- **2 teaspoons soft brown sugar**
- **2 tablespoons soy sauce**

PEANUT SAUCE:

- **125 g/4 oz dry roasted peanuts**
- **2 garlic cloves, chopped roughly**
- **1 hot fresh red chilli, deseeded and chopped roughly**
- **2.5 cm/1 inch piece of fresh root ginger, chopped roughly**
- **300 ml/½ pint canned coconut milk**
- **300 ml/½ pint water**
- **juice of 2 limes**
- **2 teaspoons soft brown sugar**

1 To make the marinade, combine the onion, garlic, sugar and soy sauce in a shallow dish. Add the chicken strips and stir well to coat. Cover and marinate for at least 1 hour, preferably overnight.

2 To make the peanut sauce, put the peanuts in a food processor or blender with the garlic, chilli and ginger, work until finely and evenly ground, then transfer to a saucepan and add the coconut milk, water, lime juice and sugar. Simmer over a moderate heat, stirring frequently, for 10–15 minutes or until a thick sauce is obtained. Remove from the heat.

3 Thirty minutes before cooking the chicken, soak 12 bamboo skewers in warm water to cover. Drain.

4 Thread the chicken strips on to the soaked bamboo skewers. Put the skewers on the grid over hot charcoal on the barbecue. Cook, turning often, for 5–8 minutes until the chicken is charred on the outside and no longer pink on the inside.

5 Meanwhile, reheat the peanut sauce and turn into a serving bowl. Serve the satay hot as a starter or snack, with the peanut sauce for dipping. Diced cucumber and compressed rice or bean curd are traditional accompaniments.

Serves 4–6

Preparation time: 20 minutes, plus marinating

Cooking time: about 30 minutes

VARIATION

Turkey Satay

Replace the chicken with turkey breast fillets and proceed as in the main recipe. For a quick-and-easy satay sauce, put 4 heaped tablespoons crunchy peanut butter in a saucepan with 300 ml/ ½ pint water, juice of ½ lemon, 1 tablespoon each soy sauce and soft brown sugar and 1 teaspoon chilli powder. Bring to the boil, stirring constantly, then simmer gently for 5 minutes.

Hot and Sour Chicken Soup

A soup from China – full of flavour with the slightly chewy dried shiitake mushrooms contrasting with the chicken, fresh ginger and the spring onions.

- **15 g/½ oz dried shiitake mushrooms**
- **2.1 litres/3½ pints hot Chicken Stock (see pages 8–9)**
- **2 tablespoons soy sauce**
- **2 tablespoons rice wine or dry sherry**
- **1 fresh green chilli, deseeded and chopped very finely**
- **5 cm/2 inch piece of fresh root ginger, shredded very finely**
- **1 teaspoon soft brown sugar**
- **about 250 g/8 oz skinned and boned cooked chicken, shredded finely**
- **6 spring onions, shredded finely**
- **2 carrots, grated**
- **salt and pepper**
- **fresh coriander leaves, to garnish (optional)**

1 Soak the dried shiitake mushrooms in warm water to cover for about 20 minutes. Drain and reserve the soaking liquid. Thinly slice the reconstituted mushrooms.
2 Bring the stock to the boil in a large saucepan over a moderate heat. Add the reserved mushroom liquid, the soy sauce, rice wine or sherry, chilli, ginger and sugar. Lower the heat, add the mushrooms and simmer for 20 minutes.
3 Add the chicken, spring onions and carrots and simmer for a further 5 minutes. Add salt and pepper to taste and serve hot, garnished with coriander leaves, if liked.

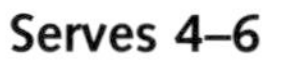

Serves 4–6
Preparation time: 10 minutes, plus soaking
Cooking time: about 25 minutes

Peking Duck

- 1 x 2 kg/4 lb oven-ready duck
- 4 tablespoons soft brown sugar
- 2 tablespoons soy sauce
- 2 tablespoons runny honey

PANCAKES:

- 125 g/4 oz plain flour
- about 125 ml/4 fl oz boiling water
- rapeseed oil, for frying

TO SERVE:

- plum or hoisin sauce
- ½ cucumber, cut into very thin matchstick strips
- 6 spring onions, cut into 5 cm/2 inch lengths and shredded finely

1 Remove fat inside the duck. Rinse the duck inside and out under cold running water. Pat thoroughly dry, inside and out, with paper towels.
2 Tie string around the neck flap of the duck. Lower the bird into a large saucepan of boiling water for about 1 minute or until the skin is taut.
3 Remove from the water, then hang up by the string over a dish. Leave to dry in a cool airy place for 2 hours.
4 Roast, breast-side up, on a rack in a roasting tin at 190°C (375°F), Gas Mark 5 for 30 minutes.
5 For the pancakes, sift the flour into a bowl, add the boiling water a little at a time, and beat vigorously with a wooden spoon after each addition until a stiff dough is formed. Cover with a cloth and let stand for at least 20 minutes.
6 Combine the sugar, soy sauce and honey and brush all over the duck. Continue roasting for 1½ hours or until the skin is crisp, dry and golden.
7 When cooked, transfer the duck to a board and let stand for 15 minutes.
8 Make the pancakes: break the dough into 8 pieces with floured hands and roll each into a ball. On a lightly floured surface, roll each ball out to a 15 cm/6 inch round.
9 Heat a little oil in a small frying pan. Add a pancake and fry for 1–2 minutes on each side until puffed up and lightly coloured. Slide on to a warm plate and cover with a damp cloth. Repeat with the remaining pancakes, brushing the pan with more oil between each and stacking them on top of each other under the damp cloth.
10 Remove the string from the duck, slice off the crisp skin and cut it into thin strips. Slice the meat into thin strips. Arrange the skin and meat together on a warmed serving plate.
11 Serve the duck with pancakes, plum or hoisin sauce, cucumber and spring onions on separate plates. Put a little sauce on a pancake, add crispy skin, meat, cucumber and spring onions. Roll up and eat.

Serves 3–4
Preparation time: 45 minutes, plus air-drying
Cooking time: 2 hours
Oven temperature: 190°C (375°F), Gas Mark 5

Chicken Teriyaki

The ideal pan for this dish is a ridged cast-iron griddle or skillet. If you do not have either of these you could use a heavy-bottomed frying pan instead.

- **2 tablespoons rapeseed oil**
- **4 large boneless chicken breast portions, skinned**
- **1 large dessert pear, peeled, cored and grated**

TERIYAKI SAUCE:

- **4 tablespoons Japanese soy sauce (shoyu)**
- **4 tablespoons Japanese rice wine (sake)**
- **2 tablespoons cold water**
- **1 tablespoon caster sugar**

TO GARNISH:

- **a few sprigs of mint**
- **radish halves**

1 Make the teriyaki sauce. Put all the ingredients in a small saucepan and heat gently, stirring, until the sugar has dissolved.

2 Heat the oil in a griddle or frying pan, add the chicken breasts and fry over a moderate heat, pressing down hard with a fish slice to keep them as flat as possible, for about 5 minutes or until they have changed colour. Turn the chicken over and repeat on the other side.

3 Pour the sauce over the chicken and let it bubble, then add the grated pear and stir well to mix. Cook over a gentle heat for 20 minutes or until the chicken is tender when pierced with a skewer or fork. Turn the chicken over and baste with the sauce several times during cooking.

4 Transfer the chicken with a slotted spoon to warmed dinner plates. Boil the sauce to reduce slightly, then spoon over the chicken. Garnish with the mint and radishes. Serve hot, with white steamed or boiled rice.

Serves 4

Preparation time: 15 minutes

Cooking time: about 30 minutes

Chicken Tikka Masala

Chicken Tikka Masala is simply Chicken Tikka cooked in the usual way (see page 60), then simmered briefly in a creamy sauce. It is mild in flavour and rich and creamy, which makes it very popular.

- **Chicken Tikka (see page 60), marinated and threaded on to skewers but not cooked**
- **2 tablespoons chopped fresh coriander**
- **juice of ½ lime**

MASALA SAUCE:

- **50 g/2 oz ghee or butter**
- **2 onions, sliced thinly**
- **2.5 cm/1 inch piece of fresh root ginger, chopped finely**
- **2 garlic cloves, crushed**
- **6 cardamom pods, bruised**
- **2 teaspoons garam masala**
- **2 teaspoons ground coriander**
- **1 teaspoon chilli powder, or to taste**
- **300 ml/½ pint double cream**
- **2 tablespoons tomato purée**
- **4 tablespoons hot water**
- **½ teaspoon sugar**
- **salt**

TO GARNISH:

- **coriander leaves**
- **slices of lime**

1 To make the masala sauce, melt the ghee or butter in a large flameproof casserole, add the onions, ginger and garlic and fry over a gentle heat, stirring frequently, for 5 minutes or until softened but not coloured.

2 Add the spices and fry, stirring, for 1–2 minutes until fragrant, then add the cream, tomato purée, water, sugar and salt to taste. Bring slowly to the boil over a moderate heat, stirring, then lower the heat and simmer gently, stirring occasionally, for 10–15 minutes. Remove the pan from the heat and leave to stand while cooking the chicken.

3 Barbecue or grill the Chicken Tikka according to the recipe instructions on page 60, then remove the cubes of chicken from the skewers.

4 Add the chicken to the masala sauce, return to a low heat and simmer, stirring, for about 5 minutes. Add the coriander and lime juice and stir again. Serve hot, garnished with the coriander leaves and slices of lime, and accompanied by either plain boiled white rice, chapattis or naan bread.

Serves 4

Preparation time: 20 minutes, plus marinating

Cooking time: 40–45 minutes

Tandoori Chicken

Instructions are given here for cooking the chicken on the barbecue for authentic-looking charred chicken, but it can be cooked under the grill. Small clay tandoori ovens are available at specialist kitchenware shops, but they do not achieve the same results as the ones in restaurants which cook at searingly high temperatures.

- **1 fresh hot red chilli, deseeded and chopped roughly**
- **2 garlic cloves, chopped roughly**
- **2.5 cm/1 inch piece of fresh root ginger, chopped roughly**
- **2 tablespoons lemon juice**
- **1 tablespoon coriander seeds**
- **1 tablespoon cumin seeds**
- **2 teaspoons garam masala**
- **6 tablespoons natural yogurt**
- **a few drops each of red and yellow food colouring**
- **½ teaspoon salt**
- **4 chicken portions, skinned**

TO GARNISH:

- **lemon wedges**
- **coriander sprigs**

1 Put the chilli, garlic, ginger and lemon juice in an electric spice mill with the whole spices and garam masala and work to a paste.
2 Transfer the spice paste to a shallow dish in which the chicken will fit in a single layer. Add the yogurt, food colouring and ½ teaspoon salt and stir to mix. Set aside.
3 Score the flesh of each chicken portion deeply with a sharp pointed knife, cutting right down as far as the bone. Put the chicken in a single layer in the dish, then spoon the marinade over the chicken and brush it into the cuts in the flesh. Cover and marinate in the refrigerator for at least 4 hours, preferably overnight.
4 Put the chicken on the grid over hot charcoal on the barbecue. Cook, turning often, for 30 minutes or until the juices run clear when the thickest part of a portion is pierced with a fork. Serve hot, garnished with lemon wedges and coriander sprigs, and accompanied by a salad of shredded lettuce, white cabbage and raw onion slices, a sauce made of yogurt and chopped mint, and plain naan bread.

Serves 4
Preparation time: 20 minutes, plus marinating
Cooking time: 30 minutes

VARIATION

Chicken Tikka

Replace the chicken portions with 4 large boneless chicken breast portions, skinned and cut into cubes, then proceed as in the main recipe. After marinating, thread the cubes of chicken on to kebab skewers. Place the skewers on the grid over hot charcoal on the barbecue (or under the grill) and cook, turning the skewers often, for 10–15 minutes until the chicken juices run clear.

Chicken Korma

Moghul korma dishes from Northern India are rich, creamy and mild in flavour, which is why they are so popular in the West. This recipe is finished off with cream and almonds, making it luxuriously flavoured.

- **3 tablespoons ghee or butter**
- **1 onion, chopped finely**
- **2.5 cm/1 inch piece of fresh root ginger, crushed**
- **2 garlic cloves, crushed**
- **5 cm/2 inch cinnamon stick**
- **4 cardamom pods, bruised**
- **4 cloves**
- **2 teaspoons garam masala**
- **1 teaspoon turmeric**
- **½ –1 teaspoon chilli powder, according to taste**
- **12 skinned and boned chicken thighs, cut into bite-sized pieces**
- **300 ml/½ pint double cream**
- **50 g/2 oz ground almonds**
- **salt**
- **toasted flaked almonds, to garnish**

1 Melt the ghee or butter in a large flameproof casserole, add the onion, ginger and garlic and fry gently, stirring often, for about 5 minutes until softened but not coloured.

2 Add the whole and ground spices and salt to taste. Fry, stirring, for 1–2 minutes, then add the chicken and stir well to coat in the spice mixture. Increase the heat to moderate and fry, stirring frequently, for about 10 minutes until the chicken changes colour on all sides.

3 Cover the casserole and simmer over a very gentle heat, stirring occasionally, for 20 minutes.

4 Add the cream and ground almonds. Stir well to mix. Simmer uncovered, stirring often, for 10 minutes or until the chicken is tender. If the curry becomes too thick, thin it with a few spoonfuls of water. Remove the whole spices, if you like, then taste and add more salt and chilli powder if necessary. Serve hot, garnished with toasted flaked almonds.

Serves 4

Preparation time: 20 minutes

Cooking time: about 40 minutes

Sag Chicken

'Sag' means spinach in Indian cookery. It is a popular vegetable in curries, because it takes on the flavour of garlic and spices so well. Here, the chicken and spices are fried with a little natural yogurt to begin with. This is a technique worth borrowing for other curries as it helps give a creamy texture to the sauce.

- **2 tablespoons ghee or butter**
- **2 onions, sliced thinly**
- **2 garlic cloves, crushed**
- **1 tablespoon black mustard seeds**
- **2 teaspoons ground coriander**
- **2 teaspoons ground ginger**
- **1 teaspoon chilli powder**
- **1 teaspoon turmeric**
- **1 kg/2 lb skinned and boned chicken thighs, cut into bite-sized pieces**
- **125 ml/4 fl oz natural yogurt**
- **100 ml/3½ fl oz water**
- **500 g/1 lb fresh young spinach, stalks removed**
- **salt**

1 Melt the ghee or butter in a large flameproof casserole, add the onions and garlic and fry over a gentle heat, stirring frequently, for 5 minutes until softened but not coloured.

2 Add the spices and salt to taste. Fry, stirring, for 1–2 minutes until fragrant, then add the chicken and stir well to coat in the spice mixture. Increase the heat to moderate and fry, stirring frequently, for about 10 minutes or until the chicken has changed colour on all sides.

3 Add half the yogurt, increase the heat to moderate and fry, stirring, for 5 minutes or until all of the yogurt has been absorbed.

4 Stir in the water, add ½ teaspoon salt, cover and simmer over a gentle heat, stirring frequently, for about 20 minutes.

5 Add the spinach, stir well to mix, cover and simmer for a further 10 minutes, or until the spinach has wilted and the chicken is cooked and feels tender when pierced with either a fork or skewer. Taste and then add more salt if necessary. Serve hot, drizzled with the remaining yogurt.

Serves 4

Preparation time: 15–20 minutes

Cooking time: 50–55 minutes

Chicken Dhansak

Dhansak recipes always include lentils among their ingredients and the meat is always served off the bone, together with saffron or pilau rice.

- **250 g/8 oz yellow split lentils**
- **900 ml/1½ pints water**
- **2 tablespoons ghee or butter**
- **4 chicken portions, skinned**
- **1 large onion, chopped finely**
- **2 garlic cloves, chopped finely**
- **2 teaspoons garam masala**
- **1 teaspoon turmeric**
- **1 teaspoon hot chilli powder**
- **½ teaspoon ground cloves**
- **4 large ripe tomatoes, skinned, deseeded and chopped roughly**
- **salt**

1 Put the lentils and water in a large saucepan, add 1 teaspoon salt and bring to the boil over a moderate heat. Lower the heat, cover and simmer gently for 30 minutes or until lentils are tender and have absorbed most of the water.
2 Meanwhile, melt the ghee or butter in a large flameproof casserole, add the chicken and sauté for 7–10 minutes over a moderate heat until golden on all sides. Remove with a slotted spoon and set aside on a plate.
3 Add the onion, garlic and spices to the casserole and fry over a gentle heat, stirring frequently, for about 5 minutes until softened. Add the tomatoes and salt to taste and stir well to mix. Return the chicken to the casserole with the juices that have collected on the plate and spoon over the vegetables.
4 When the lentils are cooked, pour them over the chicken and shake the casserole vigorously so that they mix into the spiced vegetables. Add a little water if the mixture seems dry. Cover and simmer over a gentle heat, stirring occasionally, for 30 minutes or until the chicken is tender when pierced with a skewer or fork.
5 Remove the casserole from the heat. Lift the chicken out of the lentil mixture and leave until cool enough to handle.
6 Remove the chicken from the bones and cut the meat into bite-sized pieces. Return the chicken to the casserole and reheat for 5 minutes or so. Taste, and add salt if necessary. Serve hot, with saffron rice.

Serves 4
Preparation time: 20 minutes
Cooking time: about 1 hour

VARIATION

Chicken Curry with Chick Peas and Potatoes

Make the curry according to the main recipe, but with the following differences: omit the lentils. Replace the chicken portions with 1 kg/2 lb skinned and boned chicken thighs, cut into bite-sized pieces. Proceed as in the main recipe, adding a 1 x 425 g/14 oz can chick peas, drained, and 2 medium potatoes, cut into chunks, with the tomatoes in step 3. Proceed as in the main recipe, omitting steps 5 and 6. Adjust the seasoning to taste, then serve.

Chicken Biryani

For the authentic Indian look and flavour, use basmati rice, with its unique, subtle taste. It is delicate and a little difficult to cook, so do follow these instructions carefully.

- **50 g/2 oz ghee or butter**
- **1 onion, sliced thinly**
- **2 garlic cloves, crushed**
- **2 teaspoons garam masala**
- **1 teaspoon ground coriander**
- **1 teaspoon chilli powder**
- **1 teaspoon turmeric**
- **500 g/1 lb skinned and boned chicken thighs, cut into small bite-sized pieces**
- **400 ml/14 fl oz cold water**
- **375 g/12 oz basmati rice**
- **6 cardamom pods, bruised**
- **300 ml/½ pint boiling water**
- **salt**
- **fresh coriander leaves, to garnish**

1 Melt the ghee or butter in a large flameproof casserole, add the onion and garlic and fry over a gentle heat, stirring frequently, for 5 minutes or until softened but not coloured.
2 Sprinkle in the ground spices and salt to taste. Fry gently, stirring, for 1–2 minutes until fragrant, then add the chicken and stir to coat in the spice mixture.
3 Gradually add the cold water, stirring all the time, and bring slowly to the boil over a moderate heat. Lower the heat, cover and simmer, stirring occasionally, for 20 minutes.
4 Meanwhile, rinse the basmati rice in several changes of cold water until the water is almost clear, then put the rice in a medium saucepan with the bruised cardamom pods and ½ teaspoon salt. Pour in the boiling water, then immediately cover the pan with a tight-fitting lid and cook the rice over a gentle heat, without lifting the lid, for 7 minutes.
5 Uncover the rice, fork through very gently, then add to the chicken in the pan and stir gently to mix all the ingredients. Cover and continue cooking over a gentle heat for about 10 minutes longer or until the chicken is tender. Taste and add more salt if necessary.
6 Pile the biryani on to a warmed serving platter and garnish with coriander leaves. Serve immediately. A plain or cucumber raita would be a good accompaniment, or a tomato and raw onion sambal.

Serves 4–6
Preparation time: 20 minutes
Cooking time: about 35 minutes

Balti Chicken

Balti dishes from Northern India are named after the vessel in which they are cooked – a pot rather like a wok.

- ½ teaspoon black peppercorns
- ½ teaspoon nigella seeds
- ½ teaspoon fennel seeds
- 2 tablespoons rapeseed oil
- 1 onion, sliced thinly
- 2.5 cm/1 inch piece of fresh root ginger, crushed
- 1 garlic clove, crushed
- 1 tablespoon garam masala
- 1 teaspoon ground coriander
- 1 teaspoon ground cumin
- 1 teaspoon chilli powder, or to taste
- 1 teaspoon turmeric
- 475 ml/16 fl oz water
- 50 g/2 oz coconut milk powder
- 1 tablespoon lemon juice
- 6 cardamom pods, bruised
- 5 cm/2 inch cinnamon stick
- 1 bay leaf
- 1 kg/2 lb skinned and boned chicken thighs, cut into bite-sized pieces
- 4 ripe tomatoes, skinned, deseeded and chopped roughly
- ¼ teaspoon sugar
- salt
- fresh coriander leaves, to garnish

1 Dry-fry the peppercorns, nigella and fennel seeds in a wok or large deep frying pan over a gentle heat, stirring constantly, for 2–3 minutes until fragrant, then pound to a fine powder in a mortar and pestle.

2 Heat the oil in the same pan, add the onion, ginger and garlic and fry gently, stirring frequently, for about 5 minutes until soft but not coloured.

3 Add the spice powder, garam masala, coriander, cumin powder, chilli powder and turmeric. Stir-fry for 2–3 minutes, then add the water, coconut milk powder, lemon juice and ½ teaspoon salt. Bring to the boil, stirring, then add the cardamoms, cinnamon and bay leaf. Simmer, stirring occasionally, for 15–20 minutes, until a glaze forms on the liquid.

4 Add the chicken, tomatoes and sugar and stir well. Cover and cook over a gentle heat for 40 minutes, stirring occasionally, or until the chicken feels tender when pierced with a fork or skewer.

5 Remove and discard the bay leaf and cinnamon stick, then taste, and add more salt if necessary. Serve hot, sprinkled with fresh coriander leaves, and accompanied by chapattis, puris or naan bread.

Serves 4–6

Preparation time: 30 minutes

Cooking time: 40 minutes

Coq au Vin

- 1 x 2 kg/4 lb oven-ready chicken, giblets removed, cut into 8 pieces
- 2 teaspoons dried thyme
- 3 tablespoons rapeseed oil
- 175 g/6 oz rindless smoked streaky bacon rashers, chopped
- 16 small pickling onions, blanched and peeled
- 250 g/8 oz small button mushrooms
- 3 garlic cloves, crushed
- 3 tablespoons Cognac
- 350 ml/12 fl oz red wine
- 1 bouquet garni
- 1 tablespoon butter
- 2 tablespoons plain flour
- salt and pepper

TO GARNISH (OPTIONAL):

- fresh thyme
- fresh parsley

1 Rub the chicken with the dried thyme and pepper to taste. Sauté half the pieces in the oil in a large flameproof casserole for 7–10 minutes until golden. Remove with a slotted spoon and set aside on a plate. Repeat with the remaining chicken.
2 Add the bacon to the casserole and cook over a moderate heat, stirring frequently, until the fat runs. Add the onions, mushrooms and garlic and cook, stirring frequently, for 5 minutes.
3 Return the chicken and its juices to the casserole. Gently warm the Cognac in a small saucepan, set it alight with a match, then pour it carefully over the chicken. When the flames subside, add the wine, and bring to the boil, stirring. Add the bouquet garni and salt and pepper to taste. Cover and simmer over a gentle heat, stirring occasionally, for 40 minutes or until the chicken is tender when pierced with a fork.
4 Remove the chicken and vegetables with a slotted spoon and keep hot. Discard the bouquet garni. Mix the butter and flour to a paste and add to the sauce a little at a time until evenly blended. Bring to the boil and simmer, stirring constantly, for 2–3 minutes until the sauce thickens. Adjust the seasoning to taste.
5 Serve the chicken and vegetables with the sauce spooned over, and garnished with thyme and parsley, if using.

Serves 4
Preparation time: 30 minutes
Cooking time: about 50 minutes

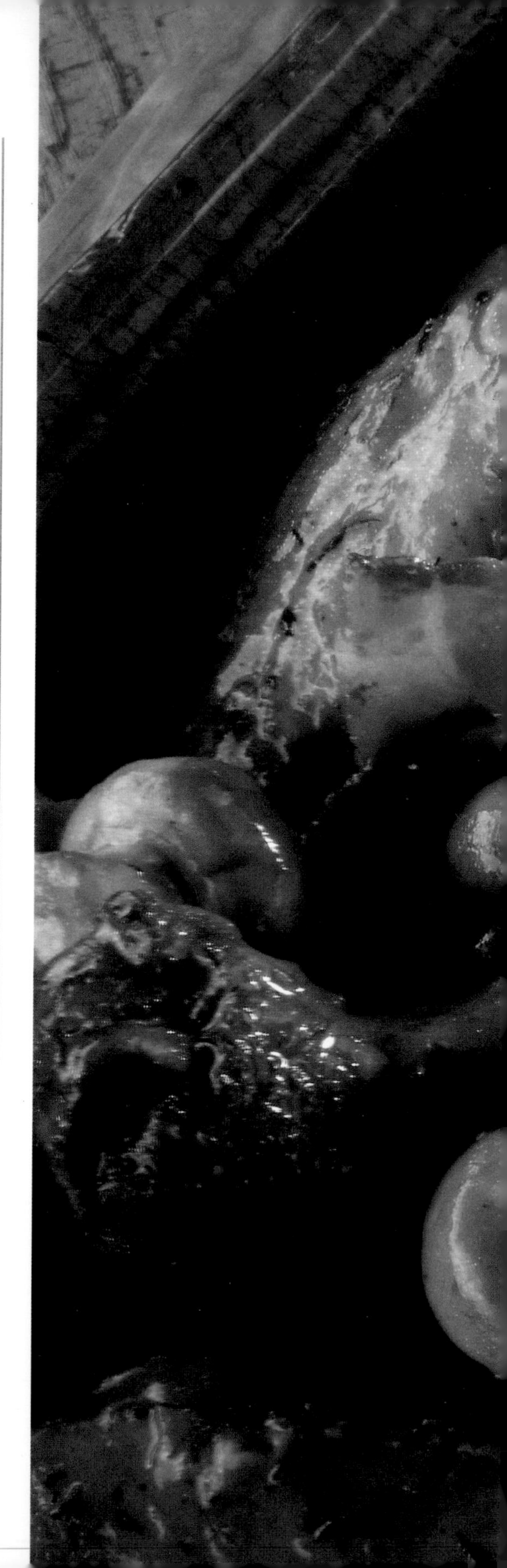

Chicken Couscous

This stew from North Africa is the ultimate one-pot dish.

- **125 g/4 oz chick peas, soaked in cold water overnight, then drained**
- **2 onions, chopped finely**
- **3 garlic cloves, chopped finely**
- **2 teaspoons ground coriander**
- **2 teaspoons cumin**
- **2 teaspoons turmeric**
- **2 teaspoons chilli powder**
- **2 tablespoons virgin olive oil**
- **2 tablespoons tomato purée**
- **12 skinned and boned chicken thighs, cut into large bite-sized pieces**
- **500 g/1 lb couscous**
- **½ teaspoon ground cinnamon**
- **few drops of orange flower water**
- **4 carrots, sliced thickly**
- **2 parsnips, sliced thickly**
- **2 potatoes, cut into chunks**
- **50 g/2 oz butter**
- **4 courgettes, sliced thickly**
- **2 tablespoons sultanas or raisins**
- **a few drops harissa sauce, to taste**
- **salt and pepper**
- **fresh coriander, to garnish**

1 Simmer the chick peas in boiling water for 1 hour. Drain.
2 Gently fry the onions, garlic and ground spices in the oil in the bottom of a couscousière or large saucepan, for about 5 minutes until softened.
3 Stir in the tomato purée, chick peas and seasoning. Cover with water and bring to the boil, stirring. Simmer, stirring occasionally, for 1 hour. Top up with water to keep the chick peas covered. Add the chicken pieces, cover and simmer for 20 minutes, stirring occasionally.
4 Meanwhile, put the couscous in a bowl and cover with boiling water. Add the cinnamon and orange flower water and stir.
5 Stir the carrots, parsnips and potatoes into the chicken and chick peas, cover with water and bring to the boil.
6 Put the couscous and half the butter in the steamer on top of the couscousière (or in a fine-meshed sieve over the saucepan). Cover and cook for 30 minutes or until the chicken and vegetables are tender, adding the courgettes and sultanas or raisins halfway through.
7 Remove the couscous, check the chicken for seasoning, add harissa sauce to taste and stir well.
8 Fork the remaining butter into the couscous and arrange in a ring on a dish with the chicken and vegetables in the centre. Garnish with coriander and serve extra harissa separately.

Serves 6–8
Preparation time: 40 minutes, plus soaking
Cooking time: about 2¾ hours

Catalan Chicken

Catalonia, in the north-east of Spain, is the home of this unusual but delicious dish. With the addition of bitter chocolate to the sauce, it has similarities with the Mexican dish, Turkey Mole (see page 72).

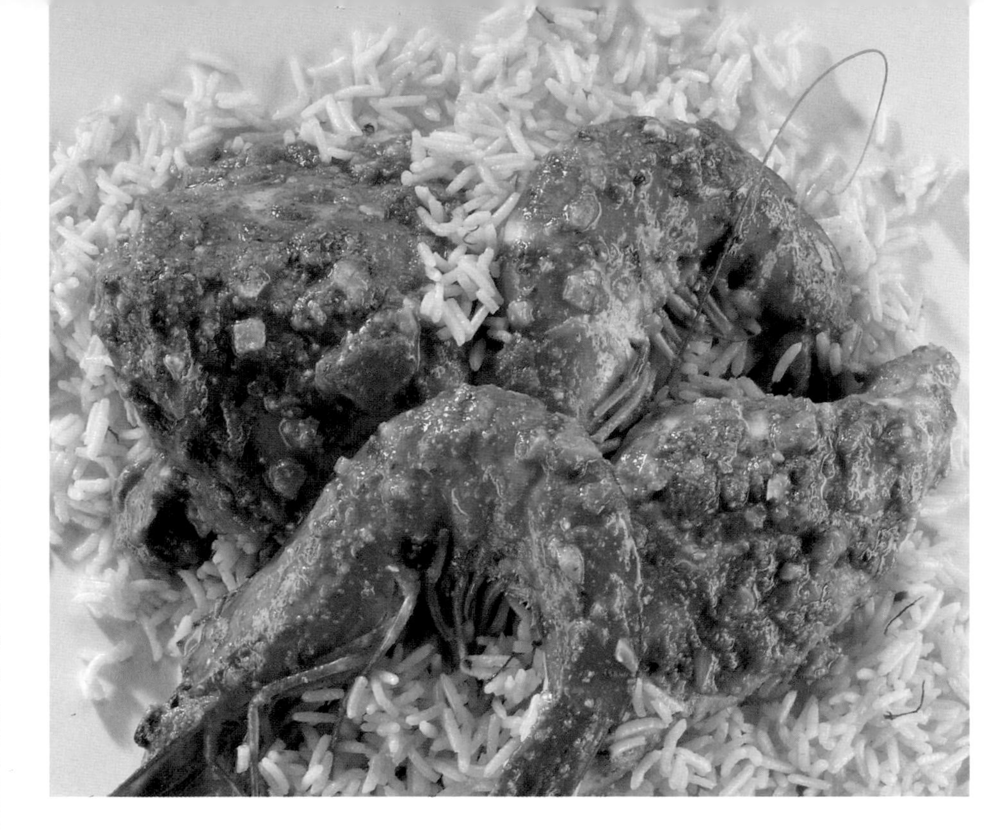

- **2 tablespoons virgin olive oil**
- **1 x 2 kg/4 lb oven-ready chicken, giblets removed, cut into 8 pieces**
- **125 ml/4 fl oz brandy**
- **1 onion, chopped finely**
- **2 large ripe tomatoes, peeled, deseeded and chopped roughly**
- **125 ml/4 fl oz cold water**
- **8 raw Dublin Bay or other jumbo prawns in their shells**
- **salt and pepper**

PICADA:

- **2 tablespoons virgin olive oil**
- **liver from the chicken, chopped roughly (optional)**
- **1 thick slice of white bread, crusts removed, broken into pieces**
- **2 garlic cloves, chopped roughly**
- **20 blanched almonds, chopped roughly**
- **15 g/½ oz bitter chocolate, chopped roughly**
- **2 tablespoons chopped fresh parsley**
- **1 tablespoon plain flour**
- **about 4 tablespoons hot water**

1 First make the picada. Heat the oil in a small frying pan, add the chicken liver, if using, the bread and garlic and fry over a moderate heat, stirring all the time, for 5 minutes.

2 Turn the fried mixture into a food processor or blender, add the remaining picada ingredients and work to a thick paste, adding more hot water if necessary. Set aside.

3 Heat the oil in large flameproof casserole, add the chicken pieces and sauté over a moderate heat for 7–10 minutes until golden on all sides. Remove from the heat.

4 Gently warm the brandy in a small saucepan, set it alight with a match, then pour it carefully over the chicken. When the flames have died down, remove the chicken with a slotted spoon and set it aside on a plate.

5 Return the casserole to the heat, add the onion and fry gently, stirring frequently, for about 5 minutes or until softened. Add the tomatoes and salt and pepper to taste and cook gently, stirring frequently, for about 5 minutes.

6 Add the picada and water and stir well to mix. Return the chicken pieces to the casserole with all the juices that have collected on the plate. Spoon over the liquid to cover the chicken, adding more hot water if necessary.

7 Cover the casserole and simmer over a gentle heat, stirring occasionally, for 30 minutes or until the chicken is tender when pierced with either a skewer or fork.

8 Add the prawns and cook for a further 5 minutes or until they turn pink. Taste the sauce for seasoning and adjust if necessary. Boiled saffron rice is the only accompaniment needed for this rich dish, with perhaps a simple lettuce salad tossed in a tangy oil and vinegar dressing to refresh the palate afterwards.

Serves 4

Preparation time: 40 minutes
Cooking time: 40–45 minutes

Turkey Mole

This Mexican dish includes a little bitter chocolate in its sauce. Used in many Mexican sauces, chocolate adds body, colour and richness.

- **1 x 1–1.25 kg/2–2½ lb boned turkey breast joint**
- **4 tablespoons rapeseed oil**
- **2 bay leaves**
- **2 onions, chopped finely**
- **3 garlic cloves, chopped finely**
- **2 tablespoons sesame seeds**
- **salt and pepper**

MOLE SAUCE:

- **1 x 425 g/14 oz can chopped or crushed tomatoes**
- **25 g/1 oz raisins**
- **25 g/1 oz unblanched almonds, chopped roughly**
- **1 slice of white bread, crusts removed and broken into pieces**
- **1 corn tortilla, broken into pieces (optional)**
- **2 hot fresh green or red chillies, deseeded and chopped roughly**
- **½ teaspoon fennel seeds**
- **½ teaspoon ground cinnamon**
- **¼ teaspoon ground aniseed**
- **¼ teaspoon ground cloves**
- **40 g/1½ oz bitter chocolate, coarsely grated**

1 Fry the turkey in half the oil in a flameproof casserole, turning often, for about 10 minutes until evenly browned. Add the bay leaves, with half the chopped onions and garlic. Cover the turkey with cold water and add salt and pepper to taste.

2 Bring to the boil, cover and simmer over a gentle heat for about 1½ hours until the turkey is tender.

3 To make the mole sauce, put the remaining onions and garlic in a food processor with all the sauce ingredients, except the chocolate. Process, adding a little turkey liquid to blend the mixture if necessary.

4 When the turkey is cooked, remove it and strain the liquid into a jug. Leave the turkey until cool enough to handle, then shred it. Remove and discard all skin and fat.

5 Heat the remaining oil in the casserole, add the sauce mixture and cook, stirring constantly, for 5 minutes or until dark in colour. Add the chocolate, mix until melted, and gradually add enough cooking liquid to make a thick, runny sauce. Stir and simmer for 15 minutes or until the sauce is rich and dark, adding more of the cooking liquid as necessary. Check the seasoning.

6 Heat the turkey in the sauce for about 5 minutes. Meanwhile, put the sesame seeds in a small frying pan and dry-fry over a gentle heat for 2–3 minutes until toasted golden.

7 Serve hot, garnished with toasted sesame seeds. Traditional accompaniments are boiled white rice, flour tortillas, chopped coriander and fresh chillies, sliced radishes, chopped onions and tomatoes.

Serves 4–6

Preparation time: 30 minutes

Cooking time: 2½–2¾ hours

Spanish Paella

- 1 kg/2 lb fresh mussels
- 4 garlic cloves
- 1 bunch of fresh mixed herbs
- 150 ml/¼ pint dry white wine
- about 2 litres/3½ pints hot Chicken Stock (see pages 8–9) or water
- 4 small squid, cleaned and sliced into rings
- 4 tablespoons virgin olive oil
- 1 large onion, chopped finely
- 1 red pepper, cored, deseeded and chopped
- 4 large ripe tomatoes, skinned, deseeded and chopped
- 12 skinned and boned chicken thighs, cut into bite-sized pieces
- 500 g/1 lb short-grain rice
- 125 g/4 oz fresh or frozen peas
- 12 large raw prawns, peeled (optional)
- salt and pepper
- chopped parsley, to garnish

1 Scrub the mussels with a stiff brush and scrape off the beards and barnacles with a small sharp knife. Discard any open mussels.

2 Slice 2 garlic cloves and crush the remainder. Put the slices in a large saucepan with the herbs, wine, 150 ml/¼ pint stock or water and season to taste. Add the mussels, cover the pan tightly and bring to the boil. Shake the pan and simmer for 5 minutes until the mussels open. Remove the mussels from the liquid and set aside, discarding any which remain closed. Strain the liquid and reserve.

3 Sauté the squid in half the oil for 5 minutes, stirring frequently.

4 Add the onion, red pepper and crushed garlic and cook gently, stirring frequently, for 5 minutes until softened. Add the mussel cooking liquid, tomatoes and seasoning. Bring to the boil, stirring, then simmer over a gentle heat, stirring, for 15–20 minutes until the mixture is thick. Transfer to a bowl.

5 Sauté the chicken in the remaining oil for 5 minutes. Add the rice and turn it in the oil for a few minutes. Stir the squid mixture into the pan. Add about one third of the remaining stock and bring to the boil, stirring.

6 Boil rapidly for 3–4 minutes, cover and simmer for 30 minutes. Add more stock as the rice becomes dry and stir frequently, moving the rice into the centre so it cooks evenly. The paella is ready when the chicken is tender, the rice is al dente and almost all the liquid absorbed.

7 Check seasoning, add the peas and prawns, if using, and simmer, stirring, for 5 minutes or until cooked, adding stock or water if required.

8 Arrange the mussels decoratively on top of the paella, cover tightly with foil and cook for 5 minutes or until the mussels are hot. Sprinkle with parsley, and serve.

Serves 6

Preparation time: about 40 minutes

Cooking time: about 1¼ hours

Italian Pot-roast Turkey with Risotto Stuffing

- 1 onion, chopped finely
- 2 tablespoons virgin olive oil
- 125 g/4 oz risotto rice
- 900 ml/1½ pints hot Chicken Stock (see pages 8–9)
- 125 g/4 oz rindless pancetta or smoked streaky bacon rashers, chopped
- 1 medium fennel bulb, chopped finely, with feathery fronds reserved
- 2 garlic cloves, chopped finely
- 50 g/2 oz Parmesan cheese, freshly grated
- 1 egg, beaten
- 1 x 3 kg/6 lb oven-ready turkey, giblets removed
- 15 g/½ oz butter
- 4 tablespoons anise-flavoured liqueur
- 150 ml/¼ pint dry white wine
- salt and pepper

1 Gently fry the onion in half the oil in a saucepan, stirring, until softened but not coloured.
2 Stir in the rice, add half the stock and bring to the boil. Stir until the stock is absorbed, then add the remaining stock and return to the boil. Cover and simmer, stirring frequently, for 15 minutes or until all the stock is absorbed. Set aside.
3 Gently fry the pancetta or bacon in another pan until the fat starts to run. Add the fennel, garlic and pepper to taste and cook, stirring, for 10 minutes until soft. Add to the rice with half the Parmesan and the egg. Stir, check seasoning and leave to cool.
4 Wash and dry the turkey cavity and sprinkle with salt and pepper. Fill the neck end with stuffing and truss with string. Place any leftover stuffing in an oiled baking dish and sprinkle with the remaining Parmesan.
5 Heat the remaining oil and butter in a flameproof casserole into which the turkey will just fit. Add the turkey and cook for about 10 minutes until lightly coloured on all sides.
6 Pour the liqueur over the turkey, allow to sizzle, then pour over the wine and season to taste.
7 Cover and cook in a preheated oven, 180°C (350°F), Gas Mark 4 for 2½-3 hours until the juices run clear when the thickest part of a thigh is pierced with a skewer or fork. Baste occasionally. Place the dish of stuffing in the oven for the last 15-20 minutes, until heated through.
8 Remove the bird, cover tightly with foil and set aside to rest for about 15 minutes. Discard the trussing string. Keep the cooking juices hot.
9 Serve the turkey garnished with the reserved fennel fronds, with the cooking juices and any stuffing handed separately. Julienne of carrots in a cream sauce or the Italian vegetable dish of spinach tossed with pine nuts and raisins would make excellent accompaniments.

Serves 6–8
Preparation time: 50 minutes
Cooking time: 2½–3 hours
Oven temperature: 180°C (350°F), Gas Mark 4

Pollo alla Cacciatora

Porcini – Italian dried mushrooms – are available at most delicatessens and some good supermarkets. Though expensive, they are full of flavour, so you need only a very small quantity.

- 15 g/½ oz dried mushrooms
- 150 ml/¼ pint warm water
- 2 tablespoons virgin olive oil
- 4 chicken portions, skinned
- 1 onion, chopped finely
- 1 large carrot, chopped finely
- 1 large celery stick, chopped finely
- 2 garlic cloves, crushed
- 150 ml/¼ pint Italian dry white wine
- 1 x 425 g/14 oz can peeled plum tomatoes
- 1 tablespoon tomato purée
- 1 teaspoon dried oregano
- 1 teaspoon dried mixed herbs
- large pinch of sugar
- salt and pepper
- chopped fresh flat leaf parsley, to garnish

1 Soak the dried mushrooms in the warm water in a bowl for 20 minutes.
2 Meanwhile, heat the oil in a large flameproof casserole, add the chicken and sauté over a moderate heat for 7–10 minutes until golden on all sides. Remove with a slotted spoon and set aside on a plate.
3 Add the onion, carrot, celery and garlic to the casserole and fry over a gentle heat, stirring frequently, for 7–10 minutes until softened.
4 Drain the mushrooms and reserve the soaking liquid. Chop or slice the mushrooms finely.
5 Add the mushrooms to the casserole with the reserved soaking liquid and the wine, increase the heat to moderate and stir until bubbling. Add the tomatoes with their juice, stir well with a wooden spoon to break them up, then add the tomato purée, herbs, sugar and salt and pepper to taste.
6 Return the chicken to the casserole with the juices that have collected on the plate. Cover and simmer over a gentle heat, stirring occasionally, for 40 minutes or until the chicken is tender when pierced with a skewer or fork. Adjust the seasoning to taste. Serve hot, sprinkled with chopped fresh parsley. Hot ciabatta bread, together with a rocket salad, lightly tossed in a vinaigrette dressing, would be perfect accompaniments.

Serves 4
Preparation time: 20 minutes
Cooking time: about 50 minutes

Pollo alla Valdostana

Fontina is a mountain cheese from the Val d'Aosta in Northern Italy.

- **6 part-boned chicken breasts, skinned**
- **½ teaspoon dried oregano**
- **½ teaspoon dried basil**
- **2 tablespoons virgin olive oil**
- **3 thin slices of Parma ham (prosciutto di Parma), total weight about 75 g/3 oz**
- **2 garlic cloves, crushed**
- **2 tablespoons balsamic vinegar**
- **6 tablespoons dry Italian vermouth or white wine**
- **3 thin slices of Fontina cheese, total weight about 75 g/3 oz**
- **salt and pepper**
- **basil sprigs, to garnish**

1 Sprinkle the slit in each chicken breast with the dried herbs and add salt and pepper to taste.
2 Heat the oil in a large sauté pan. Add the chicken breasts and sauté over a moderate heat for 1–2 minutes on each side until they just change colour. Remove with a slotted spoon and leave until cool enough to handle. Reserve the oil.
3 Cut the slices of Parma ham in half. Stuff each chicken breast with a piece of ham, then place the breasts in a single layer in a lightly oiled ovenproof dish.
4 Return the pan to the heat, add the garlic and balsamic vinegar and stir until sizzling. Stir in the vermouth or wine. Pour over the chicken breasts.
5 Halve each slice of Fontina cheese, and put a slice on top of each chicken breast.
6 Place in a preheated oven, 200°C (400°F), Gas Mark 6 for 20 minutes or until the Fontina melts and the chicken is tender. Add pepper and serve hot, with sauté potatoes and green beans or a green salad. Garnish with basil.

Serves 6
Preparation time: 15 minutes
Cooking time: about 25 minutes
Oven temperature: 200°C (400°F), Gas Mark 6

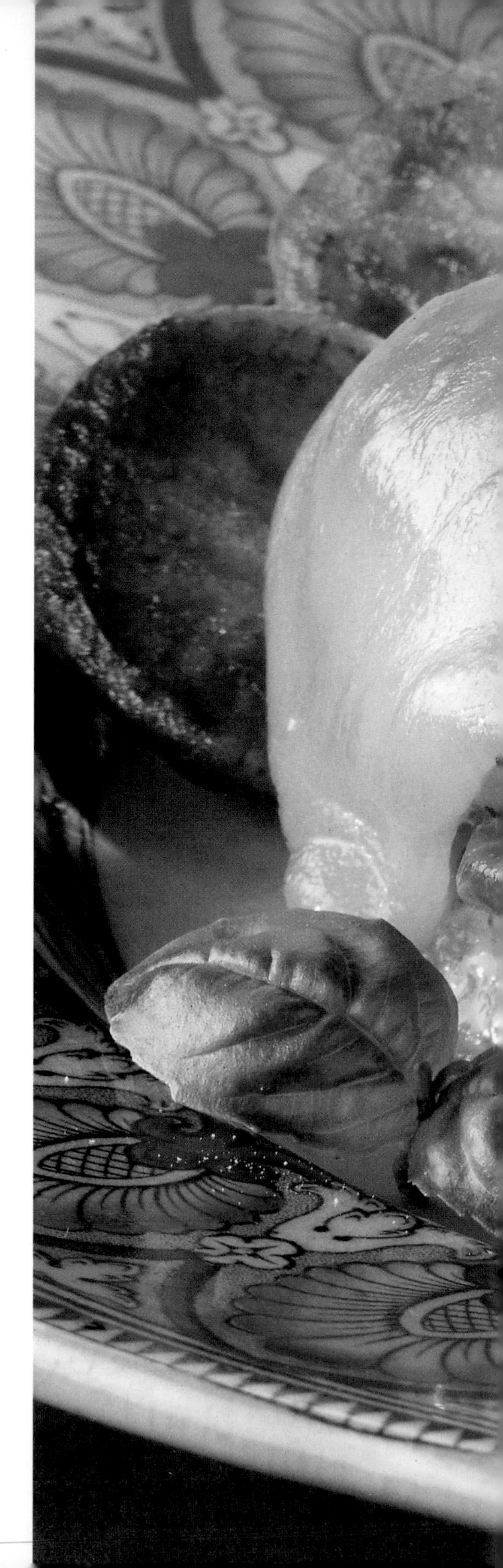

Special Occasions

Sicilian Chicken

2 tablespoons virgin olive oil
4 chicken portions, skinned
1 onion, chopped finely
1 fresh or dried red chilli, deseeded and chopped finely
1 garlic clove, crushed
25 g/1 oz sun-dried tomatoes in oil, chopped roughly
250 g/8 oz mushrooms, sliced thinly
300 ml/½ pint passata
150 ml/¼ pint dry white wine
1 teaspoon dried mixed herbs
½ teaspoon dried oregano or basil
salt and pepper

1 Heat the oil in a large flameproof casserole, add the chicken and sauté over a moderate heat for 7–10 minutes until golden on all sides. Remove with a slotted spoon and set aside on a plate.

2 Add the onion, chilli and garlic to the pan and fry, stirring frequently, for about 5 minutes until softened. Stir in the sun-dried tomatoes and mushrooms and fry for a further 5 minutes, then add the passata, white wine, herbs and salt and pepper to taste. Bring to the boil, stirring, then return the chicken to the casserole with the juices that have collected on the plate. Cover and simmer for 40 minutes or until the chicken is tender when pierced with a skewer or fork. Adjust the seasoning to taste. Serve hot, with pasta tossed in olive oil and fresh herbs.

Serves 6
Preparation time: 20 minutes
Cooking time: about 50 minutes

Roast Duck with Fresh Orange and Cointreau Sauce

- **1 x 2.75–3.25 kg/5½–6½ lb oven-ready duck, giblets removed**
- **2 teaspoons plain flour**
- **150 ml/¼ pint Chicken Stock (see pages 8–9)**
- **finely grated zest of 1 large orange**
- **juice of 2 large oranges**
- **3 tablespoons Cointreau or other orange-flavoured liqueur**
- **salt and pepper**

TO GARNISH:

- **fresh orange slices**
- **fresh watercress or bay leaves**

1 Weigh the duck and calculate the cooking time, allowing 25 minutes per 500 g/1 lb.
2 Pat the bird dry both inside and out with paper towels. Place the duck, breast-side up, on a rack in a roasting tin. Prick the skin all over with a skewer or fork and then rub all over with salt.
3 Place in a preheated oven, 190°C (375°F), Gas Mark 5 for the calculated cooking time, increasing the temperature to 200°C (400°F), Gas Mark 6 for the last 10 minutes.
4 Remove the duck from the rack, place on a warmed serving platter and cover tightly with foil. Set aside to rest in a warm place while making the sauce.
5 Pour off all but about 1 tablespoon fat from the roasting tin and set the tin on top of the stove. Sprinkle in the flour and cook over a gentle heat, stirring, for 1–2 minutes until golden. Gradually stir in the stock and bring to the boil over a moderate heat, stirring all the time. Lower the heat, add the orange zest and juice, the Cointreau and salt and pepper to taste. Simmer, stirring, for a few minutes or so until the sauce thickens. Taste for seasoning, then pour into a warmed sauce boat.
6 Serve the duck whole, garnished with orange slices and a bouquet of fresh watercress or sprigs of fresh bay leaves. Serve the sauce separately.
A dish of creamed potatoes or gratin dauphinois would be a perfect accompaniment, as would a seasonal green vegetable, such as mangetouts, broccoli or French beans.

Serves 4
Preparation time: 30 minutes
Cooking time: about 2½ hours
Oven temperatures: 190°C (375°F), Gas Mark 5, then 200°C (400°F), Gas Mark 6

Roast Duckling with Cherry Sauce

Fresh cherries are best for this dish, but their season is very short. Out of season, you can use a 425 g/14 oz can of cherries, but be sure to drain off all of the sweet syrup before cooking or it will spoil the flavour of the finished sauce.

- **6 duckling portions, each weighing about 175 g/6 oz**
- **salt and pepper**

CHERRY SAUCE:

- **375 g/12 oz fresh cherries, pitted**
- **150 ml/¼ pint dry white wine**
- **finely grated zest and juice of 1 lemon**
- **1 teaspoon caster sugar**
- **2 teaspoons cornflour**
- **2 tablespoons water**
- **4 tablespoons kirsch**
- **fresh cherries, to garnish**

1 Prick the skin of the duckling portions all over with a skewer or fork and rub with salt. Put the portions, skin-side up, on a rack in a roasting tin. Place in a preheated oven, 190°C (375°F), Gas Mark 5 for 40 minutes, increasing the temperature to 200°C (400°F), Gas Mark 6 for the last 10 minutes.

2 Meanwhile, prepare the cherry sauce. Put the cherries in a saucepan with the wine, lemon zest and juice, sugar and salt and pepper to taste. Bring to the boil over a moderate heat, then lower the heat, cover the pan and simmer for about 10 minutes until the cherries are just tender. Remove from the heat and set aside.

3 When the duckling is cooked, remove from the rack, cover and keep warm. Pour off all but about 1 tablespoon fat from the roasting tin and set the tin on top of the stove.

4 Blend the cornflour with the water in a small jug. Strain the cooking liquid from the cherries into the roasting tin and bring to the boil over a moderate heat. Pour in the cornflour mixture and simmer, stirring, for a few minutes or so until the sauce thickens. Add the kirsch and cherries and heat through gently. Taste for seasoning. Serve the duckling hot, coated with the cherry sauce and garnished with fresh cherries if available. Mangetout would make an attractive accompaniment, together with baby new potatoes or roast potatoes.

Serves 6

Preparation time: 15 minutes

Cooking time: 40 minutes

Oven temperatures: 190°C (375°F), Gas Mark 5, then 200°C (400°F), Gas Mark 6

Chicken Suprêmes with Roast Peppers

Roasting the peppers under the grill gives them a wonderful smoky flavour – a barbecue will make them taste even smokier.

- **4 sweet peppers in different colours**
- **3 tablespoons virgin olive oil**
- **4 chicken suprêmes or part-boned chicken breasts, skinned**
- **1 onion, sliced thinly**
- **2 garlic cloves, crushed**
- **50 g/2 oz sun-dried tomatoes in oil, sliced thinly**
- **2 teaspoons chopped fresh basil**
- **a few tablespoons dry white wine**
- **salt and pepper**
- **basil sprigs, to garnish**

1 Roast the peppers under a hot grill, turning frequently, for 15 minutes or until the skins blacken and blister on all sides. Remove from the grill and place each one immediately in a plastic bag. Tie each bag securely, then leave until the peppers are cold – at least 4 hours or overnight.

2 Unwrap the peppers and, one by one, hold under cold running water and rub off the blackened skins with your fingers. Pull off the stalks, slit open the peppers and remove the cores and seeds. Pat the peppers thoroughly dry with paper towels, then cut them lengthways into thin strips with a sharp knife.

3 Heat the oil in a sauté pan, and sauté the chicken over a moderate heat for 7–10 minutes until golden. Remove and set aside on a plate.

4 Add the onion slices to the pan and fry over a gentle heat, stirring frequently, for about 5 minutes or until softened but not coloured.

5 Add the roast pepper strips, the garlic, sun-dried tomatoes, basil and salt and pepper to taste. Stir well to mix, and moisten with wine. Return the chicken to the pan with the juices that have collected on the plate and spoon the pepper mixture over the top. Cover and cook for 20 minutes or until the chicken is tender when pierced with a fork, turning the chicken over and basting with the cooking liquid during this time.

6 Adjust the seasoning to taste and serve hot, garnished with basil sprigs. Polenta (boiled, grilled or fried) would make the perfect side dish, followed by a simple green salad tossed in a dressing made with olive oil and balsamic vinegar.

Serves 4

Preparation time: 30 minutes, plus cooling

Cooking time: about 45 minutes

Chicken Pancakes

- 50 g/2 oz butter
- 1 small onion, chopped very finely
- 250 g/8 oz button mushrooms, sliced
- 250 g/8 oz skinned and boned cooked chicken, shredded
- 3 tablespoons finely chopped fresh parsley
- 25 g/1 oz plain flour
- 600 ml/1 pint milk
- 150 ml/¼ pint double cream
- salt and pepper
- 25 g/1 oz Parmesan cheese, freshly grated

PANCAKES:

- 125 g/4 oz plain flour
- 1 egg, beaten
- 300 ml/½ pint milk
- 3–4 tablespoons rapeseed oil

1 Make the pancake batter. Sift the flour into a bowl with a pinch of salt. Make a well in the centre and put in the egg. Add the milk, whisking hard and drawing in the flour from the sides of the well. Set aside to rest.
2 Melt half the butter in a saucepan, add the onion and fry over a gentle heat, stirring, for 5 minutes or until softened. Add the mushrooms, increase the heat, and fry, stirring frequently, for 5 minutes or until the mushrooms soften and the juices run. Remove from the heat and turn into a bowl. Stir in the shredded chicken, 2 tablespoons of the chopped parsley and seasoning to taste.
3 Cook the pancakes. Add 1 tablespoon oil to the batter and whisk to combine. Heat about 2 teaspoons oil in a crêpe pan until very hot. Pour in a small ladleful of batter, swirl around the base of the pan and cook for about 1 minute until the pancake is golden brown on the underside.
4 Toss the pancake over and cook until golden brown on the other side, then turn the pancake out of the pan so that the side that was cooked first is underneath. Repeat with the remaining batter to make 12 pancakes altogether, adding more oil as necessary. As the pancakes are made, stack them on top of each other.
5 To make the sauce, melt the remaining butter in the pan in which the mushrooms were cooked, sprinkle in the flour and cook over a moderate heat, stirring, for 1–2 minutes. Remove the pan from the heat and slowly add 450 ml/¾ pint of the milk, beating with a balloon whisk or wooden spoon after each addition.
6 Return the pan to the heat and bring to the boil, stirring all the time. Lower the heat and simmer, stirring, for about 5 minutes until smooth.
7 Remove the pan from the heat and pour about half the sauce into the chicken and mushroom filling. Fold gently to mix and taste for seasoning.
8 Put a good spoonful of filling in the centre of each pancake and roll up into a cigar shape.
9 Stir the remaining milk and the cream into the remaining sauce in the pan and season to taste. Return to the heat and beat until hot. Pour one-third of the sauce into an oven-proof dish and spread evenly.
10 Arrange the filled pancakes in a single layer in the dish and pour over the remaining sauce. Sprinkle with Parmesan. Place in a preheated oven, 190°C (375°F), Gas Mark 5 for 20 minutes until bubbling. Serve hot, with with a green salad.

Serves 4–6
Preparation time: about 1 hour
Cooking time: 20 minutes
Oven temperature: 190°C (375°F), Gas Mark 5

Chicken Foie Gras

Pâté de foie gras is available in small cans from delicatessens. It is a good-quality pâté, excellent for making a quick sauce, but you can experiment with other pâtés, either smooth or coarse-textured, according to taste. Serve the chicken and sauce as soon as it is ready – don't let it bubble away once cooked or the sauce will separate.

- **1 tablespoon rapeseed oil**
- **25 g/1 oz unsalted butter**
- **6 boneless chicken breast portions, skinned**
- **2 tablespoons pink peppercorns, crushed**
- **200 ml/7 fl oz rosé wine**
- **200 ml/7 fl oz water**
- **1 x 125 g/4 oz can pâté de foie gras**
- **150 ml/¼ pint double cream**
- **salt and pepper**

TO GARNISH:

- **small radicchio leaves**
- **oak leaf lettuce leaves**

1 Heat the oil and butter in a large sauté pan, add the chicken and sauté over a moderate heat for about 5 minutes until golden on all sides.

2 Add the peppercorns and salt and pepper to taste, then pour in the wine and water and stir to mix with the juices in the pan. Cover and simmer over a gentle heat for 15 minutes or until the chicken is tender when pierced with a skewer or fork, turning the chicken over and basting with the cooking liquid occasionally during this time.

3 Meanwhile, mash the pâté in a bowl and gradually work in the cream until evenly mixed.

4 Remove the chicken from the pan with a slotted spoon, set aside and keep warm.

5 Increase the heat and boil the cooking liquid for a few minutes or so until reduced, then add the pâté and cream mixture and stir until evenly mixed with the liquid in the pan. Allow to bubble and thicken, then taste for seasoning.

6 Either serve the chicken with the sauce poured over, or return the chicken to the pan with the juices that have collected on the plate, and heat through gently, basting with the sauce. Serve immediately, garnished with radicchio and oak leaf lettuce, and accompanied by new potatoes and a seasonal green vegetable such as courgettes or broccoli.

Serves 6

Preparation time: 10 minutes

Cooking time: about 25 minutes

Spiced Roast Chicken

In this Indian-inspired dish, the spiced yogurt forms a dark, crisp crust contrasting with the moist and succulent white meat.

- **2 garlic cloves, chopped roughly**
- **2.5 cm/1 inch piece of fresh root ginger, chopped roughly**
- **1–2 dried red chillies, chopped roughly**
- **1 tablespoon cumin seeds**
- **1 x 500 g/1 lb carton natural yogurt**
- **2 teaspoons turmeric**
- **1 teaspoon dried mint**
- **½ teaspoon ground mixed spice**
- **1 x 2 kg/4 lb oven-ready chicken, giblets removed**
- **⅓ cucumber, cut into very thin matchstick strips**
- **2 tablespoons chopped fresh mint**
- **salt**
- **fersh mint sprigs, to garnish**

1 Put the garlic, ginger, chillies and cumin seeds in a food processor with about half the yogurt, the turmeric, dried mint, mixed spice and ½ teaspoon salt. Work until all the ingredients are finely ground and evenly mixed into the yogurt – the mixture will be quite runny.

2 Wash inside the chicken and dry thoroughly with paper towels. Slash the skin through to the flesh with a sharp pointed knife, then truss the chicken with string.

3 Put the bird into a large bowl and pour the yogurt mixture all over. Cover and leave to marinate for at least 8 hours or overnight, turning the chicken from time to time.

4 Put the chicken in an ovenproof dish into which it just fits. Place in a preheated oven, 180°C (350°F), Gas Mark 4 for 2–2¼ hours or until the juices run clear when the thickest part of a thigh is pierced with a skewer or fork. Baste frequently and spoon over half the remaining yogurt halfway through the roasting time.

5 Remove the bird, cover tightly with foil and set aside to rest. Keep the cooking juices hot.

6 Make a simple cucumber raita by mixing the remaining yogurt with the cucumber, chopped mint and salt to taste. Turn into a serving bowl.

7 Remove the trussing string and discard. Put the chicken on a warmed serving platter and, if liked, pour on some or all of the cooking juices, or pour them into a small jug to be served separately. Garnish the chicken with mint and serve with the cucumber raita. Basmati rice would make another ideal accompaniment, with a dish of curried vegetables, and a sambal salad of diced beetroot, onion and yogurt.

Serves 4

Preparation time: 15 minutes, plus marinating
Cooking time: 2–2¼ hours
Oven temperature: 180°C (350°F), Gas Mark 4

Chicken Gloria

- 2 tablespoons virgin olive oil
- 1 medium Spanish onion, chopped finely
- 1 ripe large (beefsteak) tomato, skinned and chopped roughly
- 2 garlic cloves, crushed
- 1 x 2 kg/4 lb corn-fed chicken, cut into 8 pieces and skinned, or 4–6 chicken portions, skinned
- 4 tablespoons mushroom soup powder
- 4 tablespoons cold milk
- 450 ml/¾ pint Spanish Champagne (cava) or sparkling dry white wine
- 200 ml/7 fl oz double cream
- salt and pepper
- finely chopped fresh flat-leaf parsley, to garnish

1 Heat the oil in a large flameproof casserole, add the onion, tomato and garlic and cook gently, stirring frequently, for about 10 minutes.
2 Add the chicken, season to taste and sauté over a moderate heat for 7–10 minutes until the chicken changes colour on all sides.
3 Mix the mushroom soup powder to a 'cream' with the milk.
4 Add the Champagne or wine, cream and mushroom cream to the chicken and stir well to mix. Cover and simmer over a gentle heat for 30 minutes or until the chicken is tender, turning the chicken over and basting with the cooking liquid frequently during this time.
5 Taste the sauce for seasoning. Transfer the chicken to warmed plates and coat with the sauce. Garnish with parsley and serve.

Serves 4
Preparation time: 15 minutes
Cooking time: about 50 minutes

VARIATION

Chicken and Prawns with Italian Sauce

1 Heat 2 tablespoons virgin olive oil in a large flameproof casserole, add 1 small onion, chopped finely, and 1 garlic clove, crushed, and cook gently, stirring, for 5 minutes.
2 Add 4 skinned chicken portions, season to taste, and sauté for 7-10 minutes until the chicken has changed colour on all sides.
3 Add 1 x 425 g/14 oz can chopped tomatoes with Italian herbs, stir well to mix, then pour in 300 ml/½ pint Champagne or sparkling dry white wine and stir again. Cover and simmer over a gentle heat for 30 minutes until the chicken is tender when pierced with a skewer or fork, turning the chicken over and basting with the cooking liquid frequently during this time.
4 Add 250 g/8 oz cooked peeled prawns to the casserole and stir well to mix. Heat through for a few minutes, then taste the sauce for seasoning. Serve hot, sprinkled with chopped fresh flat leaf parsley.

Serves 4
Preparation time: 15 minutes
Cooking time: about 50 minutes

Poussins Guiolle

- **2 x 500 g/1 lb poussins**
- **4 garlic cloves, cut into slivers**
- **1 lemon, quartered**
- **3 heaped tablespoons runny honey**
- **2 tablespoons butter**
- **½–1 teaspoon hot chilli powder**
- **1 teaspoon paprika**
- **450 ml/¾ pint hot chicken stock made with a stock cube**
- **½ teaspoon crushed chillies**
- **salt and pepper**

1 Make several incisions in the flesh of the poussins with a small sharp knife and insert the garlic slivers into them. Place 2 lemon quarters in the cavity of each poussin, then place both the poussins on a rack in a roasting tin.
2 Put 2 tablespoons of the honey in a small saucepan with the butter, chilli powder and paprika. Heat gently until melted, then brush all over the poussins and sprinkle with salt and pepper to taste.
3 Pour about half the stock into the tin, then place in a preheated oven, 190°C (375°F), Gas Mark 5 for 20 minutes.
4 Mix the remaining honey and stock with the crushed chillies, pour into the tin and continue roasting for about 20–25 minutes until the juices run clear when the thickest part of a thigh is pierced with either a skewer or fork. Serve the poussins hot, with the sauce poured over, accompanied with a fresh green vegetable such as mangetout or French beans.

Serves 2
Preparation time: 10 minutes
Cooking time: about 50 minutes
Oven temperature: 190°C (375°F), Gas Mark 5

VARIATION

Poussins with Goats' Cheese and Herbs

1 Lift up the skin at the neck end of each of 2 x 500 g/1 lb poussins and carefully work your fingers between the skin and the breast flesh to make a 'pocket'.
2 Mash 125 g/4 oz goats' cheese and mix with 2 tablespoons chopped fresh herbs, 1 garlic clove, crushed, and pepper to taste.
3 Push the cheese mixture into the pockets in the poussins, then place on a rack in a roasting tin. Brush all over the birds with 25 g/1 oz softened butter and sprinkle with pepper.
4 Place in a preheated oven, 190°C (375°F), Gas Mark 5 for 40–45 minutes until the juices run clear when the thickest part of a thigh is pierced with a fork. Serve the poussins hot, garnished with fresh herbs.

Serves 2
Preparation time: 10 minutes
Cooking time: 40–45 minutes
Oven temperature: 190°C (375°F), Gas Mark 5

Chicken with White Wine, Gruyère and Mushrooms

- **4 part-boned chicken breasts, skinned**
- **50 g/2 oz unsalted butter**
- **½ teaspoon dried mixed herbs**
- **½ teaspoon dried tarragon**
- **250 g/8 oz button mushrooms, sliced thinly**
- **25 g/1 oz plain flour**
- **300 ml/½ pint milk**
- **150 ml/¼ pint dry white wine**
- **75 ml/3 fl oz double cream**
- **125 g/4 oz Gruyère cheese, grated**
- **good pinch of freshly grated nutmeg**
- **salt and pepper**

1 Put the chicken breasts in a single layer in an ovenproof dish, dot with half the butter, sprinkle with the herbs, and season to taste. Cover with foil and place in a preheated oven, 180°C (350°F), Gas Mark 4 for 30 minutes or until just tender when pierced with a skewer or fork.
2 Meanwhile, melt the remaining butter in a saucepan, add the mushrooms and sauté over a moderate heat, stirring frequently, for about 5 minutes until the juices run.
3 Sprinkle in the flour and cook, stirring, for 1–2 minutes. Remove the pan from the heat and add the milk a little at a time, beating with a whisk or wooden spoon after each addition. Add the wine in the same way.
4 Return the pan to the heat and bring to the boil, stirring all the time. Lower the heat and simmer, stirring, for about 5 minutes until thickened.
5 Add the cream, two-thirds of the Gruyère, the nutmeg and salt and pepper to taste, and simmer over a very gentle heat for a further 5 minutes. Remove from the heat.
6 When the chicken is tender, remove from the oven and increase the oven temperature to maximum. Tip any juices from the chicken into the sauce and stir well to mix. Pour the sauce over the chicken in the dish and sprinkle with the remaining Gruyère.
7 Return the chicken to the oven and bake for a further 5 minutes or until golden and bubbling. Serve hot, with a salad of crisp green leaves, finely sliced roast peppers and sun-dried tomatoes.

Serves 4
Preparation time: 30 minutes
Cooking time: about 35 minutes
Oven temperatures: 180°C (350°F), Gas Mark 4, then 240°C (475°F), Gas Mark 9

Chicken and Red Pesto Roulades

Red pesto, which is made from sun-dried tomatoes, pine nuts and Parmesan cheese, is more unusual than the classic green pesto made with basil, but it is now becoming more widely available in supermarkets and delicatessens. It makes an interesting alternative to tomato coulis in many dishes. If you can get purple basil for the garnish, it will complement the colours of the other ingredients.

- **6 large boneless chicken breast portions, skinned**
- **50 g/2 oz butter**
- **4 tablespoons red pesto (see recipe introduction above)**
- **12 back bacon rashers, rinds removed**
- **2 tablespoons virgin olive oil**
- **125 ml/4 fl oz red wine**
- **175 ml/6 fl oz hot Chicken Stock (see pages 8–9)**
- **4 tablespoons crème fraîche**
- **salt and pepper**

TO GARNISH:

- **cherry tomatoes**
- **fresh basil leaves**

1 Make a long horizontal slit through the thickest part of each chicken breast without cutting right through.
2 Beat the butter and pesto together in a bowl, then spread the mixture inside the cavities in the chicken breasts, dividing it equally between them. Close the chicken tightly around the pesto mixture.
3 Stretch the bacon rashers with the flat of a large knife blade, then wrap 2 bacon rashers tightly around each chicken breast, overlapping the rashers so that the chicken is completely enclosed in the bacon. Secure with wooden cocktail sticks.
4 Heat the oil in a large sauté pan, add the chicken breasts in a single layer and sauté over a moderate heat for 3 minutes on each side or until the bacon colours.
5 Add the wine and stock and bring to the boil, spooning liquid over the chicken constantly. Cover and simmer over a gentle heat for about 15 minutes until the chicken is tender when pierced with either a skewer or a fork.
6 Remove the roulades from the pan with a slotted spoon, cover and keep warm. Add the crème fraîche to the pan and boil, stirring, until the liquid is thickened and reduced to a syrupy glaze. Adjust the seasoning to taste. Serve hot, with the sauce poured over and around. Garnish with cherry tomatoes and basil.

Serves 6
Preparation time: 20 minutes
Cooking time: 20–25 minutes

Chicken Olives

- 40 g/1½ oz butter
- 175 g/6 oz fresh wild mushrooms, chopped finely
- 125 g/4 oz fresh breadcrumbs
- finely grated zest and juice of 1 lemon
- 3 tablespoons finely chopped fresh parsley
- 1 egg, beaten
- 6 large boneless chicken breast portions, skinned
- 2 tablespoons virgin olive oil
- 200 ml/7 fl oz hot Chicken Stock (see pages 8–9)
- 150 ml/¼ pint dry white wine
- 1 bouquet garni
- 125 ml/4 fl oz crème fraîche
- salt and pepper
- fresh herbs, to garnish

1 Melt 25 g/1 oz butter in a frying pan, add the mushrooms and season to taste. Sauté over a moderate heat, stirring, for 5 minutes or until the juices run. Remove from the heat.
2 Put the breadcrumbs in a bowl, add the mushrooms and their juices, the lemon zest and juice and the herbs. Stir well to mix, taste for seasoning, then bind with the beaten egg.
3 Make a long horizontal slit through the thickness of each chicken breast, without cutting right through. Open out the chicken and place between 2 sheets of greaseproof paper. Flatten the chicken by pounding it with a rolling pin.
4 Remove the paper and divide the stuffing equally between the chicken breasts, forming it into a cylinder shape along one of the edges of each breast. Roll up the chicken around the stuffing in a Swiss roll shape, tucking in the ends as you go. Secure with wooden cocktail sticks.
5 Heat the oil and remaining butter in a large flameproof casserole, add the chicken olives and fry over a moderate heat for 5–7 minutes until they have changed colour on all sides.
6 Pour in the stock and wine and bring to the boil. Add the bouquet garni, cover and simmer for 30 minutes or until the chicken feels tender when pierced with a fork. Spoon the cooking liquid over the olives and turn them occasionally during cooking.
7 Lift the chicken olives out of the cooking liquid with a slotted spoon, cover and keep warm.
8 Remove the bouquet garni from the cooking liquid and discard. Add the crème fraîche and bring to the boil, stirring constantly. Reduce the heat and simmer, stirring frequently, for about 5 minutes, until the sauce has reduced and thickened slightly. Season to taste.
9 Remove and discard the cocktail sticks from the chicken, then cut the chicken diagonally into neat, thick slices. Spoon the sauce on to warmed dinner plates, top with the chicken slices and garnish with fresh herbs. Serve immediately, with boiled rice and a green vegetable or salad.

Serves 6
Preparation time: 30 minutes
Cooking time: about 40 minutes

Chicken with 40 Garlic Cloves

A delicious traditional Provençal dish which is perfect for a Sunday lunch 'al fresco'.

- **1 x 2 kg/4 lb oven-ready, corn-fed chicken, giblets removed**
- **1 bouquet garni**
- **4 tablespoons virgin olive oil**
- **40 garlic cloves, separated but not peeled**
- **1 celery stick, chopped**
- **salt and pepper**
- **a few sprigs each of fresh rosemary, sage and thyme, to garnish**

FOR SEALING:

- **4 tablespoons plain flour**
- **4 teaspoons water**

1 Wash and dry the chicken cavity, insert the bouquet garni and add salt and pepper to taste. Truss the chicken with string.
2 Heat the oil in a large flameproof casserole into which the bird just fits. Add the garlic and celery, then the chicken and cook until it is lightly coloured on all sides.
3 Cover the casserole with its lid. Make a paste with the flour and water and use to carefully seal around the edge.
4 Place the casserole in a preheated oven, 180°C (350°F), Gas Mark 4 for 2¼ hours, without opening the oven door during cooking.
5 Break the flour and water seal, then lift out the chicken and place on a warmed serving platter. Arrange the garlic cloves around the chicken and garnish with sprigs of rosemary, sage and thyme. Serve hot, with mashed potatoes and a juicy vegetable dish such as ratatouille.

Serves 4
Preparation time: 15 minutes
Cooking time: 2¼ hours
Oven temperature: 180°C (350°F), Gas Mark 4

Pasta with Chicken, Cream and Mushroom Sauce

Use white button mushrooms for this sauce – dark ones will spoil its delicate appearance.

- **3 part-boned chicken breasts**
- **1 small onion, quartered**
- **1 carrot, chopped roughly**
- **1 bouquet garni**
- **a few black peppercorns**
- **300 ml/½ pint water**
- **2 tablespoons dry sherry (optional)**
- **50 g/2 oz butter**
- **250 g/8 oz button mushrooms, sliced thinly**
- **2 garlic cloves, crushed**
- **1 teaspoon chopped fresh rosemary**
- **1 tablespoon virgin olive oil**
- **375 g/12 oz dried pasta shapes (e.g. bows, penne or spirals)**
- **1½ tablespoons plain flour**
- **150 ml/¼ pint double cream**
- **salt and pepper**
- **fresh rosemary, to garnish**

1 Put the chicken in a saucepan with the onion, carrot, bouquet garni and peppercorns. Pour in the water and add the sherry, if using.
2 Bring to the boil, then lower the heat, cover and poach the chicken for about 20 minutes until just tender when pierced with a skewer or fork.
3 Meanwhile, melt the butter in a separate pan, add the mushrooms, garlic, rosemary and salt and pepper to taste, and sauté over a moderate heat, stirring often, for 5 minutes or until the juices run. Remove from the heat. With a slotted spoon, transfer the mushrooms from the buttery liquid to a bowl.
4 Bring a large saucepan of water to the boil, swirl in the oil and add ½ teaspoon salt. Add the pasta and boil, uncovered, over a moderate heat for 10 minutes, or according to packet instructions, until al dente.
5 Meanwhile, lift the chicken out of the poaching liquid, then strain the liquid into a jug. Cut the chicken into strips, discarding the skin and bones.
6 Return the mushroom cooking liquid to the heat, sprinkle in the flour and cook for 1–2 minutes, stirring. Add the chicken poaching liquid a little at a time, beating well after each addition.
7 Bring to the boil, stirring. Lower the heat and add the chicken, mushrooms, cream and seasoning. Stir well, then simmer, stirring, for 5 minutes or until thickened.
8 Drain the pasta and turn into a warmed serving bowl. Pour in the sauce and toss to mix with the pasta. Serve hot, garnished with rosemary.

Serves 4
Preparation time: 30 minutes
Cooking time: 30 minutes

Turkey Escalopes with Chestnut Sauce

Cans of unsweetened chestnut purée are available all year round in large supermarkets and delicatessens. At Christmas time you could use this delicious nutty sauce to cover slices of leftover roast turkey. Make the sauce as described and simply add the turkey to heat through for 5 minutes at the end.

- **6 tablespoons canned unsweetened chestnut purée**
- **300 ml/½ pint hot Chicken Stock (see pages 8–9) or water**
- **juice of 1 large orange**
- **1 teaspoon chopped fresh thyme or ½ teaspoon dried**
- **small pinch of ground cinnamon**
- **1½ tablespoons rapeseed oil**
- **4 large turkey escalopes**
- **salt and pepper**

TO GARNISH:

- **orange twists (optional)**
- **fresh thyme sprigs**

1 Put the chestnut purée in a bowl and gradually work in the stock or water, orange juice, thyme, cinnamon and salt and pepper to taste. Beat vigorously to combine.

2 Heat the oil in a large frying pan, add the turkey escalopes and sauté over a moderate heat for 1–2 minutes on each side.

3 Pour the chestnut and orange mixture over the escalopes and bring to the boil, stirring. Lower the heat, cover and simmer for 20 minutes or until the escalopes are tender when pierced with a fork, turning the escalopes over and basting with the sauce occasionally during this time.

4 Taste the dish for seasoning and add salt and pepper as necessary. Serve hot, garnished with orange twists, if using, and a few thyme sprigs. Creamed or mashed potatoes and a seasonal green vegetable, such as broccoli, courgettes or Brussels sprouts, would go extremely well with this dish.

Serves 4

Preparation time: 10 minutes

Cooking time: 15–20 minutes

Boned Rolled and Stuffed Festive Turkey

- **1 x 1–1.25 kg/2–2½ lb joint smoked pork loin**
- **1 x 3.5 kg/8 lb oven-ready turkey, dressed weight with giblets removed**
- **125 g/4 oz unsalted butter, softened**
- **salt and pepper**

STUFFING:

- **2 tablespoons rapeseed oil**
- **1 large onion, chopped finely**
- **2 celery sticks, chopped finely**
- **375 g/12 oz mixed dried fruit (apricots, prunes, apples, peaches), chopped finely**
- **375 g/12 oz fresh breadcrumbs (white or wholemeal, according to taste)**
- **250 g/8 oz mixed shelled nuts, chopped finely**
- **1 medium cooking apple, peeled, cored and grated**
- **2 tablespoons chopped fresh parsley**
- **1 tablespoon chopped fresh thyme or 2 teaspoons dried**
- **2 eggs, beaten**

GRAVY:

- **900 ml/1½ pints hot Giblet Stock (see page 9)**
- **finely grated zest and juice of 2 oranges**
- **4 tablespoons port or sherry**
- **2 tablespoons cranberry sauce or jelly**

1 First cook the pork loin. Weigh the joint and calculate the cooking time, allowing 20 minutes per 500 g/1 lb. Put the joint in a saucepan, cover with cold water and bring to the boil. Drain off the water, then cover with fresh cold water, bring to the boil again, cover and simmer for the calculated cooking time. Drain and leave to cool completely. Meanwhile, bone the turkey, either completely, or partially with some bone remaining in the legs (see page 7), and then make the stuffing.

2 To make the stuffing, heat the oil in a saucepan, add the onion and celery and fry over a gentle heat, stirring frequently, for about 10 minutes until softened. Turn into a bowl, add the remaining stuffing ingredients with salt and pepper to taste and mix well together. Set aside.

3 Put the turkey, breast-side down, on a board. Sprinkle the flesh with salt and pepper to taste, then spread with half the stuffing. Put the cold pork loin lengthways in the centre of the bird, then cover with the remaining stuffing, pushing it down into the cavities in the legs where the bones have been removed.

4 Bring the turkey up and around the pork and stuffing to enclose both of them completely, then sew along the centre seam with a trussing needle and thread.

5 Turn the turkey breast-side up and carefully ease your fingers between the skin and the flesh. Push in the softened butter to cover the breast completely, then turn the turkey over and sew up the neck and tail ends, making as neat and compact a shape as possible. Tie the legs together at the front of the turkey.

6 Put the turkey, breast-side up, in a buttered roasting tin into which it just fits (this helps it keeps its shape during roasting). Place in a preheated oven, 180°C (350°F), Gas Mark 4 and roast for 3 hours or until the juices run clear when the thickest part is pierced with a skewer or fork. Cover with foil if the skin becomes too brown during cooking.

7 Lift the turkey out of the tin, cover tightly with foil and set aside to rest in a warm place for 30 minutes. (This allows the juices to settle into the meat and makes the turkey much easier to carve.)

8 Pour off the fat from the roasting tin, leaving behind the sediment and pan juices. Set the tin over a high heat on top of the stove and pour in the giblet stock. Bring to the boil and boil until reduced by about one-third. Lower the heat to moderate, whisk in the orange zest and juice, the port or sherry, cranberry sauce or jelly and salt and pepper to taste. Simmer, stirring, for a few minutes until hot, then taste for seasoning, adjusting if necessary, and pour into a warmed gravy boat.

9 Serve the turkey and gravy hot, with all the traditional Christmas trimmings and accompaniments. Alternatively, omit the gravy and serve the turkey cold as part of a buffet meal with a selection of salads.

Serves 10–12

Preparation time: 1½–2 hours, plus cooling

Cooking time: 3 hours

Oven temperature: 180°C (350°F), Gas Mark 4

Recipe Photographer:
Alan Newnham
Recipe Home Economist:
Meg Jansz
Jacket Photographer:
Ian Wallace
Jacket Home Economist:
Sunil Vijayakar